THE REGULATED CONSUMER

$7.95

by Mary Bennett Peterson

"Nobody seriously challenges the fact that the regulatory agencies have made an accommodation with the businesses they are supposed to regulate—and that they've done so at the expense of the public."—Ralph Nader

Despite the efforts of Mr. Nader and his Raiders, Virginia Knauer, Betty Furness, and Bess Myerson, among other "consumer advocates," the consumer is being smothered by the very federal laws, regulations, and agencies promoted and set up to "protect" him. The end is right, but the means are wrong.

This is the thought-provoking point of this fully documented book that scrutinizes seven regulatory agencies and asks: What is the price of this protection?

Agencies examined closely are the Food and Drug Administration, the Antitrust Division of the Justice Department, the Federal Trade Commission, the National Labor Relations Board, the Interstate Commerce Commission, the Civil Aeronautics Board, and the Federal Communications Commission.

So where are we going in this burgeoning business of government regulation, especially at the federal level? Why are we regulating our people more and more — directly through welfare means tests, income tax regulations, minimum wages, licensing requirements, travel restrictions, the draft, the farm program, etc., and indirectly through government agencies which control and politicalize in one way or another consumers, via direct regulation over businesses, indus-

ves, the profes-
s ever-expanding
sumer choice, in-
e economic effi-
se our abundant

rson: Most regu-
c interventionism
Washington Way
free market way
e economic ver-
men rather than
he name of pro-
undermines the
imer.

, Mary Bennett
ular contributor
nal, writing the
siness." She is
erin Society, an
nomists. She is
t, and both her
graduated from
9 with majors in
ockbroker, she
ith a nonprofit

The Regulated Consumer

Mary Bennett Peterson

Nash Publishing, Los Angeles

Library of Congress Catalog Card Number: 71-153200
Standard Book Number: 8402-5002-9

Published simultaneously in the United States and
Canada by Nash Publishing, 9255 Sunset Boulevard,
Los Angeles, California 90069.

Printed in the United States of America
First printing

Preface

Consumerism is moving rapidly—the question is, moving where? Man as citizen and consumer needs government—the question is, how much? Whether government in the name of consumer protection should increasingly regulate society—i.e., consumers and producers, be they individuals or groups of individuals, such as businesses and unions—is also a tough political and economic question. How, if at all, government should regulate is an equally tough question. Perhaps this book will suggest some dimensions to these questions and hopefully encourage scholars, economists, editors, writers, government officials, men and women community leaders, businessmen and businesswomen, consumer advocates and other opinion-makers to seek fuller answers than those presented here.

My aim in this brief discussion is to focus on whether regulation is a boon or bane to the consumer. It is also to get people to look back at where we have been, where we are today, and to ask where we are going in this burgeoning business of government regulation, especially at the federal level. Why are we regulating our people more and more—directly through welfare means tests, income tax regulations, minimum wages, licensing requirements, travel restrictions, the draft, the farm program, etc., and indirectly through government agencies which control and politicize in one way or another consumers, businesses, industries, unions, cooperatives, the professions, etc.? How, then, is ever-expanding regulation affecting consumer choice, individual freedom, and the efficiency with which we use our abundant yet limited resources?

In the U. S. at least, regulation is of relatively recent date. Looking back, we see a grand design for a free society and a free economy. Under the influence of 18th-century political philosophers profoundly skeptical of the omnipotent state—Locke, Hume, Adam Smith, Montesquieu, and others—the framers of the Constitution built a political structure on a foundation of limited government. The structure was anchored to a written constitution that could be amended only by elaborate and time-consuming processes. The powers of the central government were deliberately limited in a number of other significant ways: by the principle of federalism, for example, which divided sovereignty among the political centers of the federal capital and each co-equal state capital, by the prohibition of bills of attainder and ex post facto laws, by a Bill of Rights, a bicameral legislature, a tripartite central government of three branches—legislative, executive, and judicial. All these and other checks and balances were designed to preclud a future homegrown George III or, in the words of the Declaration of Independence, "a multitude of New Offices."

Limitations on government also existed in the economic sphere. Economic decision-making in production of goods and services was left almost entirely in private hands. In this sense, the Constitution was an economic as well as a political document. What little economic regulation there was, was largely exercised by the states. About all the federal government could do, in the economic realm, was to coin money, provide for a patent system, run a post office, construct post roads, fix standards for weights and measures, levy and collect taxes and tariff duties, and "regulate Commerce with foreign Nations, and among the states, and with the Indian Tribes." This latter "commerce clause," however, has been interpreted by the Supreme Court to permit the rise of the regulatory agencies, beginning with the Interstate Commerce Commission in 1887. But such interpretation was not apparently in the purview of the designers of the Constitution. As Jefferson put it in his First Inaugural Address:

> Still one more thing, fellow citizens, a wise and frugal government, which shall restrain men from injuring one another, shall leave them otherwise free to regulate their own pursuits of industry and improvement and shall not take from the mouth of labor the bread it has earned.

Today, clearly, Washington and not Albany or Austin, Sacramento or Springfield, or even all the state capitals put together, wields *the* power. Moreover, beginning near the close of the 19th century a fourth branch was added to the federal government: the "independent" regulatory agency or commission, such as the Federal Power Commission, the Civil Aeronautics Board, and the Atomic Energy Commission.

This essay proposes to examine a sampling of the regulatory agencies, both independent and executive, with the aim of seeing how they are faring. Faring not just for themselves—for obviously the fourth branch of government survives, and then some; it could hardly do otherwise as Parkinson's First Law on the inherently expansive nature of bureaucracy postulates. But, rather, faring for the person I still consider to be the "forgotten man" in much, and I think, perhaps most, of the regulatory picture—namely, and ironically, the American consumer.

Permit a few words about this "forgotten man" phrase, a phrase borrowed from William Graham Sumner. As Yale's Professor Sumner first put it in 1883— and the basic format doesn't seem to have changed since —A and B get together to decide just what C will do for D, or for A and B. C, the Forgotten Man, has little voice in the matter; he merely pays the bills. But C, in the merry-go-round of politics, wears more than one hat, as do A, B, and D. Thus when C on occasion becomes, let us say, A, he takes his turn to do in the Forgotten Man. And this, according to Voltaire, is the art of politics: to take from some in order to give to others. One other

point: All too often B stands for businessman; businessmen have frequently been factors initiating and extend-
ing regulation of, paradoxically, business.

In the words of Sumner:[1]

> It is the Forgotten Man who is threatened by
> every extension of the paternal theory of gov-
> ernment. It is he who must work and pay.
> When, therefore, the statesmen and social phi-
> losophers sit down to think what the State can
> do or ought to do, they really mean to decide
> what the Forgotten Man shall do.

My thesis is, in brief, that well-meaning people promoting regulation all too often get the opposite of
their intentions. The consumer, nominally the object of
protection by antitrust and regulation, is the one who
frequently loses in the end, notwithstanding the recent
governmental addition of a Presidential Special Assistant for Consumer Affairs and a growing movement of
consumerism. This new movement of government and
consumer groups is predicated on the premise that consumer sovereignty is more or less defunct. Accordingly,
the movement is pressing retailers and manufacturers
for fuller labeling, tighter safety standards, better product performance, improved warranties and servicing,
and the like.

This book sets out to show that consumerism is all
too frequently a matter of right ends and wrong means.
The consumer is the one who has to pay the govern-

---

[1]*What Social Classes Owe to Each Other*, Caxton, 1952, p. 130.

mental freight of regulation; and at a greater expense
he has to pay the cost in economic inefficiency of whatever regulatory mismanagement happens to come along
—and a great deal does come along.

This is not to say, however, that all regulation is un-
welcome—as will be discussed later. Neither is it to say
that a revamping of the federal regulatory agencies as
proposed in 1971 by the President's Advisory Council
on Executive Organization, led by Roy L. Ash, is un-
welcome; yet this revamping proposal seems to miss the
point that the ultimate answer to the regulatory problem is deregulation.

So this book is essentially the story of the Washington
way—the regulatory way. Necessarily the story swings
on a limited selection of regulatory agencies for discussion; there are some fifty major ones and literally hundreds of minor ones. *The United States Government
Organization Manual,* a voluminous handbook on the
federal agencies, available from the Government Printing Office, requires more than sixty pages of fine print,
two columns to a page, just to index and cross-index all
the bureaus and agencies, regulatory and non-regula-
tory. So the reader interested in the background and
functions of, say, the Tennessee Valley Authority, Equal
Employment Opportunity Commission, Small Business
Administration, or the Federal Reserve Board will find
little or nothing on these agencies here.

With the consumer in mind, I discuss essentially but
seven agencies: the Food and Drug Administration, the
Antitrust Division of the Justice Department, the Federal Trade Commission, the National Labor Relations

Board, the Interstate Commerce Commission, the Civil Aeronautics Board, and the Federal Communications Commission. While my selection is limited and inevitably arbitrary, I believe that it still is fairly representative of regulation; and whatever valid observations I may make are, I believe, applicable as a rule to regulation anywhere—federal, state, or local, American or foreign.

So many people gave me a hand in the preparation of this volume, from supplying ideas to reading interim drafts, that I cannot name them all, and for that reason I would rather not name any. I want particularly, however, to thank my husband and children for their forbearance and cooperation. Whatever sins of omission and commission this book may contain, they are mine alone.   Mary Bennett Peterson

Princeton, New Jersey
1971

Contents

Introduction

Mary Peterson persuasively illustrates for seven selected agencies what might be called the natural history
of governmental intervention into economic affairs: a
real or fancied evil leads to demands to "do something
about it"; a political coalition forms consisting of sincere high-minded reformers and equally sincere interested parties; the incompatible objectives of the members of the coalition (e.g., low prices to consumers and
high prices to producers) are glossed over by fine rhetoric about "the public interest," "fair competition,"
and the like; the coalition succeeds in getting Congress
(or a state legislature) to pass a law; the preamble to
the law entombs the rhetoric and the body of the law
grants power to governmental officials to "do something"; the high-minded reformers experience a glow
of triumph and turn their attention to new causes; the
interested parties go to work to make sure that the

power is used for their benefit and generally succeed;
success breeds its problems, requiring the scope of intervention to broaden; bureaucracy takes its toll so that
even the initial special interests no longer benefit; ultimately, the effects are precisely the opposite of the noble
objectives of the high-minded reformers without achieving the more mundane objectives of the special interests; yet the activity is so firmly established and so many
vested interests are connected with it that repeal of the
initial legislation is nearly inconceivable; instead, new
governmental legislation is called for to cope with the
problems produced by the old; and a new cycle begins.

The oldest case considered by Mrs. Peterson is the
Interstate Commerce Commission which reveals in pris-
tine purity each of these steps—from the curious coalition that achieved its initial establishment (reformers
bewailing the evils of the railroad monopoly and railroad interests eager to have government assistance in
enforcing minimum fares) to the beginning of a second
cycle by the establishment of a nationalized passenger
corporation (Amtrak) whose only excuse for existence
is that it is largely free from ICC regulation and can
therefore do what ICC will not permit the individual
railroads to do! The rhetoric, of course, says that the
purpose of Amtrak is better rail passenger transportation, yet it is supported by the railroads because it will
permit most existing passenger service to be eliminated.

The fascination of Mrs. Peterson's admirable survey
is how closely this pattern is followed in each of the
illustrative cases she considers.

The seven-told tale raises a number of troublesome
questions.

First, who really benefits from the intervention? It is tempting to say that the owners or managers of the regulated industries do—the owners of railroads, trucking companies, trunk airlines, TV stations and networks, and so on. No doubt, some did—especially those who came in on the ground floor, when intervention was first established, or who received initial valuable franchises (such as TV licenses) without charge. But as intervention has proceeded, it is hard to see that present owners derive much benefit. Are the stockholders of the regulated trunk airlines better off than the stockholders of PSA—the intrastate California line that by a quirk is not subject to CAB regulation and hence charges lower fares from Los Angeles to San Francisco than the CAB imposes for comparable interstate flights? Is it at all clear that the owners of TV and radio stations as a whole have benefited from the denial to listeners of pay-TV?

Moreover, whatever may be the benefit to some individuals as producers, they bear costs as consumers. The owner of CBS stock pays higher fares to travel on planes than he would have to pay if competition reigned instead of the CAB. The owner of United Airlines stock is faced with a "wasteland of TV" because the FCC insists that advertising is the primary way in which TV is to be financed. And so on down the line.

Perhaps the governmental officials who administer the regulatory agencies benefit. But even that is far from clear. The elimination of intervention would increase the efficiency of the economic system. The opportunities for able men would be broadened. And most of the men who man the governmental agencies, certainly at the top, are able men. The tragedy is that their ability is now being devoted to impeding the satisfaction of human wants. Deregulation would enable these same abilities to be turned to productive use.

But if this is so, if almost everyone would benefit from deregulation, the second puzzling question arises. Why does the intervention persist?

Mrs. Peterson names one major governmental intervention that was terminated—namely, Prohibition. It was terminated because its effects were so obviously disastrous—and even then, only because the Great Depression made sweeping reform on a wider area politically feasible. I can think of one other—the postal savings system. Established in response to Populist demand, the System was limited by law to paying no more than 2 percent interest on savings deposits. As interest rates rose after World War II, postal savings deposits became more and more unattractive relative to other savings deposits and gradually shrank to zero, at which point there was no vested interest to keep the system from being repealed.

But these are clearly the exceptions, as Mrs. Peterson points out. The rule is that once a governmental agency is established, it seldom is either killed, as Prohibition was, or fades away, as Postal Savings did.

In her final chapter Mrs. Peterson refers to some of the reasons for the adoption of government intervention. These same reasons help explain its persistence: the seen vs. the unseen—the harm that would be done to present vested interests by deregulation is obvious and immediate while the good is often invisible and would

take time to occur; the concentrated interests of producers vs. the diffuse interests of consumers. But there
is one further factor: the tyranny of the status quo.
This tyranny initially worked against intervention. In
each case it took a great campaign to overcome that
tyranny in order to have the intervention legislated. But
once on the books, the tyranny works to maintain it.

An unrecognized virtue of the market vs. political
arrangement is precisely that it is far less subject to the
tyranny of the status quo. It is only necessary for one
individual to see how he can benefit from changing the
status quo for him to start to do so. In a truly free market, he does not have to get permission from anyone.
He can simply venture his own wealth; produce a new
product, for example, and start to sell it. He need persuade only the initial purchasers. He can begin small
and grow. And, equally important, he can fail to grow.

Contrast this with the political process. To adopt
some measure requires first persuading a majority before the measure can be tried. It is hard to start small,
and once started, almost impossible to fail. That is why
governmental intervention is at once so rigid and so
unstable.

Experience with governmental intervention gives little reason for optimism about either its performance or
the possibilities of repeal. Yet the outlook is not completely bleak. There is increasing recognition that governmental intervention in the name of helping the
consumer generally hurts the consumer. There is increasing dissatisfaction with centralized government
and impersonal bureaucracy. There is a growing desire

for individual freedom, for "doing one's own thing."
Perhaps we shall yet see in the 20th century (or 21st?)
a successful crusade to end government intervention
root and branch comparable to the successful crusade
in 19th-century Britain against the corn laws—a crusade that established free trade and ushered in a period
of unprecedented improvement in the lot of the working
man.

This book reflects the trend of opinion that may produce such a crusade. And it will reinforce and help
shape that trend. That is why I commend it to you.

Milton Friedman

Chicago, Illinois
April 2, 1971

I originally came to Washington with a great deal of hope that the regulatory agencies would champion the consumers' interests, but it didn't take me very long to become disillusioned. Nobody seriously challenges the fact that the regulatory agencies have made an accommodation with the businesses they are supposed to regulate—and that they've done so at the expense of the public.

—Ralph Nader
Playboy interview, October 1968

Mary Peterson persuasively illustrates for seven selected agencies what might be called the natural history of governmental intervention into economic affairs: A real or fancied evil leads to demands to "do something about it"; a political coalition forms consisting of sincere high-minded reformers and equally sincere interested parties; the incompatible objectives of the members of the coalition (e.g., low prices to consumers and high prices to producers) are glossed over by fine rhetoric about "the public interest," "fair competition," and the like; the coalition succeeds in getting Congress (or a state legislature) to pass a law; the preamble to the law entombs the rhetoric and the body of the law grants power to governmental officials to "do something"; the high-minded reformers experience a glow of triumph and turn their attention to new causes; the interested parties go to work to make sure that the power is used for their benefit and generally succeed; success breeds its problems, requiring the scope of intervention to broaden; bureaucracy takes its toll so that even the initial special interests no longer benefit; ultimately, the effects are precisely the opposite of the noble objectives of the high-minded reformers without achieving the more mundane objectives of the special interests; yet the activity is so firmly established and so many vested interests are connected with it that repeal of the initial legislation is nearly inconceivable; instead, new governmental legislation is called for to cope with the problems produced by the old; and a new cycle begins.

-from the Introduction by Milton Friedman—University of Chicago

The
Regulated
Consumer

CHAPTER I

Regulation—Consumer Boon or Bane?

We are very good at creating administrative agencies. But no sooner are they called into being than they become ends in themselves, acquire their own constituency as well as a "vested right" to grants from the Treasury, continuing support by the taxpayer, and immunity to political direction. No sooner, in other words, are they born than they defy public will and public policy.

—Peter F. Drucker
The Age of Discontinuity

As I see it, most current regulation, although growing rapidly, is inherently uneconomic—and, ironically, anti-consumer. Worse, it ultimately poses a threat to a free society. Most regulation is simply economic interventionism—the substitution of the Washington way—the public way—for the free market way—the private way. It is the economic version of government by men rather than government by law. In the name of protecting the consumer, it undermines consumer sovereignity. In the name of preserving competition, it undermines competition.

An example of governmental ideas on competition is seen in the dim view the English and American post office departments have long taken of competitive private message and express companies, which were, of course, a source of embarrassment and a drain on the hopefully exclusive business of the public system. Both national post offices responded as coercive monopolists, getting their respective governments to put forth laws and regulations ordering private competitors to cease and desist and restore thereby the idyllic state of pure monopoly. But woe to the consumer, for as Alfred Marshall, the founder of neoclassical economics, wrote in a letter on March 24, 1890, to the *Times* of London:

> In most other kinds of business the producer anticipates the wants of the consumer and invents new ways of satisfying them; in postal affairs alone the consumer has to clamor long before he gets the most simple and obvious reforms; and, indeed, in spite of his special facilities for clamoring . . . he often does not get them at all. . . . The Post Office, slothful in many directions, is vigorous only in this—that when private persons are inclined to invest their time and capital in the attempt to think out new ideas for the public benefit, the Post Office warns them to desist.

This is not to suggest that any and all regulation should be *verboten,* that government bureaucracy is a sin *per se.* Business and indeed all social cooperation will not work in a political vacuum. Indeed, anarchy is as destructive of social cooperation as is totalitarianism. Thus political organization and some bureaucracy and regulation are indispensable to modern society. Here I distinguish between interventionistic regulation and benign regulation.

Interventionistic regulation is essentially a substitute for free competition—freedom to buy and freedom to sell—and as such tends to be detrimental to efficient resource allocation—i.e., to human welfare. This is so because it tends to break down the constructive competing forces of the market—to distort normal supply and demand responses to price and profit signals, to continual technological advances, to constantly changing consumer preferences. It is manifested in such key forms as production allocation orders and price-fixing decrees. It is also manifested in the double standard of many businessmen who worship competition in the abstract but encourage anticompetitive regulation—a form of protectionism—in practice.

Benign regulation, on the other hand, is neutral or helpful insofar as competition or economic efficiency is concerned. In other words, it can make the market perform more satisfactorily. Enforcement of contractual obligations through the courts and establishment of a copyright system and a system of standard weights and measures are examples of benign and most constructive regulation. Again, police departments, state and local, benignly regulate traffic speeds and keep records of license applications, traffic violations, and the like. So, of course, some regulation and bureaucracy are as necessary in the public sector as they are in the private sector. But even benign regulation can get out of hand. Despite good intentions, it can become interventionistic—auto safety and ecological legislation, for example, can be overdone—carried to a point where costs outweigh benefits. To illustrate, it is estimated that to make smokestack emissions 100 percent free of pollutants is about twice as costly as to make the emissions 95 percent free—while the 95 percent pollutant-free emissions may be quite consistent with public health standards.

Since, as I will seek to show, interventionistic regulation inevitably subverts the market and thereby distorts supply and demand; it breeds politicking, lobbying, bureaucracy, red tape, opportunities for corruption, and sooner or later a misallocation of resources. It breeds, in a word, inefficiency; it involves, in University of Chicago economist George Stigler's phrase, meager means and noble ends. To put it mildly, such regulation is unbusinesslike, even though frequently it is aided and abetted, if not outrightly induced, by business pressure.

Perhaps worst of all, most current regulation dethrones the consumer in favor of the producer and/or the regulator. This is the rub with interventionistic regulation: For all his proclaimed Washington champions, the consumer is the one who is ultimately regulated, to his detriment.

Yet the consumer, however forgotten and frequently lost in the regulatory maze, is still very much remembered in the free market. He is still the wielder of his purse—an economic, life-and-death power to the tune of some three-quarters of a trillion dollars of after-tax disposable personal income—is still the director of our market economy and a savvy, if sometimes fickle and arbitrary, boss over the nation's shops, airlines, railroads, farms, stores, warehouses, factories, professions, and all other businesses in the country. Economists Ludwig von Mises and W. H. Hutt allude to this view of the consumer as "consumer sovereignty."

For it is the consumer, from Aunt Jane to Sears Roebuck (which in a way acts for Aunt Jane), who finally decides what is to be produced, how much, and who is to produce it. Put another way, each consumer, individual and corporate, is pretty much an economic sovereign deciding how, when, and where he will spend his funds and direct his own consumption. His sovereignty is not unlimited, however, as his purse is not unlimited. Further, he cannot direct the producer to sell a product below cost or produce it to standards beyond available technology.

So, in addition to two hundred million individual consumers, we have several million business consumers. Business consumers are allies of individual consumers. Sears, for example, sets quality standards for its merchandise and runs performance tests in its laboratories, thereby tending to reduce product failures for the benefit of Sears' customers. Similarly, General Motors, an enormous consumer of steel, subjects its purchased steel to exhaustive tests to determine the quality of each steel producer's product. And Hertz, in turn, in buying a huge fleet of new Chevrolets every model year, is a powerful check on General Motors—to the benefit of individual Chevrolet buyers. Thus producers, hungry for the consumer's funds and absolutely dependent on them for survival, have no choice but to cater to the consumer's wishes and commands, indeed, to kowtow to his whims and fancies, if not outright fantasies (witness how Hertz rental car advertising sought to "put you in the driver's seat").

Who in fact put the village blacksmith out of business, or, more recently, did in the iceman, or still more recently, the corner grocer? Many may be inclined to say that these enterpreneurs of another era were economically done in by the giants of Detroit, the huge utilities, Westinghouse and General Electric, the food chains of A & P, Safeway, Grand Union, and other corporate octopi. I would argue instead that the real economic executioner of the iceman was the consumer—the person who purchased an electric or gas refrigerator. Again, it is not Howard Johnson or the Holiday Inn which accounts for the virtual demise of the ma and pa motel that bloomed around the country during World War II and the postwar period. Rather, it is the motorist—the consumer again—who selects, better elects, the landscaped motel with the twenty-eight ice cream flavors, air conditioning, swimming pool, etc.

To be sure, the marketplace rule of *caveat emptor* has not been repealed, notwithstanding all the exertions of the special assistants for consumer affairs, the Ralph Naders, federal trade commissions, and so on. The consumer can indeed be taken at times—short-shrifted, short-weighted, short-changed, or otherwise deceived or ill-considered by a fast-talking salesman or a TV or an automobile repairman. Moreover, monopolies and cartels can come into existence for a time. But, as will be discussed in the next two chapters, these market aberrations are generally short-lived and relatively inconsequential in the highly dynamic and intensely competitive American economy. Again, to be sure, producers will enlist wily Madison Avenue to solicit consumer patronage, but the consumer still has the final say—Dun and Bradstreet's business mortality tables and the heavily advertised consumer product failures of Ford Motor's Edsel car, Campbell Soup's Red Kettle dried soup mix, and Dupont's Corfam leather-like material indicate.

The consumer, then, is usually the winner of the competitive race. Competition is his element. *Caveat vendor* is his threat. Even the Communists seem to be slowly catching on to the correlation between competition and productivity, between profits and economic growth, between Communist-capitalist trade (and other cooperation with private competitive producers) and mutual gain. In Poland, for example, the Communist regime decided in 1965 to go into a joint venture with Krupp, West Germany's industrial giant, as has more recently the Soviet regime with Fiat of Italy. Recently a group of U.S. businessmen after a trip to Moscow came away with the impression that Premier Alexei Kosygin might welcome, under certain conditions, similar U.S. joint ventures in the Soviet Union. But a Soviet invitation for a joint venture with Ford Motor was apparently upset by the Nixon Administration. Too, Yugoslavia has

been encouraging establishment of privately owned
motels and inns to serve foreign tourists along the
Adriatic seacoast.

In Russia, Professor Yevsei Liberman of Kharkov
State University seems to be something of a modern-
day Adam Smith, teaching the Russian Marxists the
joys of, if not free markets, freer markets. Increasingly,
post-Khrushchev rulers Brezhnev and Kosygin are in-
stalling profit guides and other competitive techniques
for Russian factories. Perhaps "Libermanism" may
someday represent the discovery that the customer is
always right, that competition and the profit motive
render results superior to those of bureaucratic planning. Agreed, the Communists are of course most un-
ready to install private capitalists and entrepreneurs in
Russia. But if they ever do, they will discover, if they
haven't already, that they will have exchanged one
commissar for another—the consumer commissar.

But how does the American consumer fare, directly
and indirectly, in our regulated society?

The high American standard of living is one measure.
Still, under the tutelage of such "consumerists" as Virginia Knauer, President Nixon's special assistant for
consumer affairs, and Ralph Nader, the crusading author of *Unsafe at Any Speed* (1965), the consumer is
caught up in a revolution of rising consumer expecta-
tions—a revolution perhaps destined for frustration or
worse, depending on how it proceeds. The White House
office for consumer affairs says the number of complaints it receives now runs about 2,500 a month,

compared with 1,500 a month in 1970. The Federal Trade Commission says consumer complaints directed to that agency have risen 50 percent since 1970 to an annual rate of 20,000. Furthermore, public-opinion surveys indicate an increasingly negative attitude towards big business. For example, Social Research, Inc., in 1971 found that 60 percent of consumers it polled in the Chicago area thought that "big business forgets the public welfare." This figure compares with 40 percent in 1964.

So the consumer is increasingly restive. He is asking producers, as he has done since time immemorial, "What have you done for me lately?" And he is complaining louder and longer as the consumerist movement spreads. The next chapter takes up the movement in some detail.

My concern in this book is less with direct consumer regulation and more with indirect consumer regulation —namely, with business and union regulation. I don't question the good intentions of all those who seek to protect the consumer through government interventionistic measures and agencies. I seek merely to point to the record to demonstrate how very frequently the results of similar measures and agencies have been quite different from those intended. And, while I am mainly interested in indirect consumer regulation, I note that many a consumer is directly regulated in his various consumer and nonconsumer capacities. To illustrate:

Item: A regulation of the Social Security Program limits earnings of Social Security recipients to a nominal sum per year from ages sixty-five to seventy-two on the penalty of progressive loss of Social Security benefits as that sum is exceeded.

Item: The Selective Service Program requires young men in peacetime to serve in the armed forces by the chance of a lottery, while a voluntary army with higher pay scales would draw only those who wish to serve, thereby improving morale, reducing army turnover, and minimizing career disruptions.

Item: the U.S. Post Office, a long-standing monument to deficit operations, bureaucratic inefficiency, political patronage, and debilitating divorce from the marketplace, was finally removed from direct political control by act of Congress in 1970 and put on a semi-autonomous basis. Still a far cry from marketplace discipline and still a monopoly, the new postal agency is at least free to set rates (within limits); raise funds through bond issues; bargain collectively with its employees; cut back on patronage; and, hopefully and eventually, run at a profit.

Item: The Bureau of Indian Affairs, after more than a century and billions of dollars, still "regulates" a few hundred thousand Indians on federal reservations. A recent survey of Indian conditions revealed the following: Per capita income was more than one-third less than that of the rest of the nation; unemployment was some ten times as great, averaging over 50 percent; the average age of Indians at death was 42, compared with 62 for the rest of the population.

Item: The U.S. Department of Agriculture provides subsidies for about three million farmers. After four decades and tens of billions of dollars, the department's farm programs continue to widen the gap between rich and poor farmers. According to the *New York Times* of April 4, 1970, the Salyer family of California received $1.7 million in farm subsidies in one year; the Thomas Washington family of South Carolina received slightly more than $300. Stories like this have triggered bills in Congress to limit subsidy payments. Subsidies are based primarily on the "parity" that existed between farm prices and the general price level that existed from 1910 to 1914. They require the farmer to restrict his cultivation to a certain acreage so as to prevent his supply, and hence the total food supply, from driving farm prices down. But historically, farmers have retired their least productive land and poured fertilizers on their allowed acreage, thereby usually boosting yields higher than the Washington officialdom had thought possible. The upshot has been decades of food surpluses going into government storage bins and then into school lunch, food stamp, "Food for Peace," and other programs designed in one way or another to relieve the surplus problem. The further upshot has been higher food prices and higher taxes for all consumers, notwithstanding the government's long furor over the evils of inflation—a total annual cost to the consumer of about $10 billion.

Item: The Aid to Families with Dependent Children program and other welfare programs have provided few incentives for welfare recipients to accept employment in low-paying jobs, inasmuch as welfare checks are usually decreased by the full amount of the take-home pay. Also, welfare payments are often withheld when the father is present in the household. This practice frequently leads to the abandonment of the family by the unemployed male head. Apparently, it also leads to an increase of the number of dependent children born out of wedlock.

Item: Consider, for a longer example, a casebook story of the Washington way of one consumeristic regulatory agency now deceased and unlamented. The Noble Experiment, engineered in part by a Minnesota congressman named Andrew J. Volstead, is a case of consumerism run wild. This was the time when government sought to protect consumer morality and health and said in effect, "Thou Shalt Not Drink." This was the era of Prohibition. Its regulatory agency was the Federal Prohibition Bureau whose job it was simply to regulate—in this case, essentially to stop—the liquor traffic. The job turned out to be anything but simple. It could not be simple, for in attempting to regulate the liquor business out of existence, the federal government was once again vainly trying to repeal the law of supply and demand. The repercussions were something less than salutary, especially for the consumer.

Prohibition started rather innocently. From the turn of the century the Drys steadily built up political power and were ready for a show of strength against Demon Rum when President Wilson vetoed the Volstead National Prohibition Bill in 1919, which had started out a few years earlier as a World War I food conservation measure. On the day of the Wilson veto, both the House and Senate rejected the President's fateful warnings of a federal fiasco and national scandal and overrode his veto. Later, thirty-six state legislatures ratified the new law of Prohibition, which became part of the Constitution as the Eighteenth Amendment. The language read simply enough:

> After one year from the ratification of this article, the manufacture, sale, or transportation of intoxicating liquors within, the importation thereof into, or the exportation thereof from the United States and all territory subject to the jurisdiction thereof, for beverage purposes is hereby prohibited.

So in the holy name of Temperance, what became perhaps the most intemperate era in the history of the United States began at 12:01 A.M. on January 16, 1920, as National Prohibition went into effect.

Naturally, Prohibition was hailed by the triumphant Drys as the dawn of a new era, a time of a new moral code of decency and sobriety. "The reign of tears is over," declared the nation's Number One evangelist, Dr. Billy Sunday, on the eve of Prohibition, and he added:[1]

> The slums will soon be only a memory. We will turn our prisons into factories and our jails into storehouses and corncribs. Men will walk upright now, women will smile and the children will laugh. Hell will be forever for rent.

But somehow regulatory experience did not follow this happy prognosis nor the jubilant prediction of the

---

[1]Henry Lee, *How Dry We Were*, Prentice-Hall, 1963, p. 193.

Anti-Saloon League of New York that the saloon was
dead, that America was about to enter an age of "clear
thinking and clean living." For one thing, the nation's
nightclubs and saloons, of course, didn't really disap-
pear. They, along with the "booze" industry, simply
went underground (sometimes literally) ; legitimacy became illegitimacy; the underworld moved in; and the
twenties are now remembered, quite correctly, as the
Roaring Twenties. Hardly a more strained, indeed, chaotic chapter in the long and not infrequently unhappy
relationship between regulator and consumer can be
found. The Volstead Act and the Eighteenth Amendment are evidence, if evidence is needed, that power to
enforce sobriety can involve the power to undermine
morality.

Results of the Noble Experiment were far from the
glowing ones promised. The late newspapers of January
16, 1920, reported that trucks loaded with contraband
liquor had been seized in Peoria, Illinois, and New York
City by federal agents. Other first-day accounts told of
clandestine stills being raided in Indiana and Michigan,
and the issuance of twelve warrants for arrest of violators of the liquor law in New York State.

This was only the beginning. Convictions in federal
courts, apart from those in local courts, for liquor violations in the twelve months from July 1, 1921, to June
30, 1922, totaled 37,181. By 1924, the population of
federal prisons had increased almost 100 percent over
the pre-Prohibition total. Even so, many federal prison-
ers had to be incarcerated in state and city jails to take
care of the overflow. Federal agents had arrested

313,940 suspected violators by 1926, while state and municipal law enforcement officers had arrested at least as many and probably many more.

A vast illicit and most unregulated industry on land and sea arose; the Coast Guard became known as "Carry Nation's Navy" as it pursued the sleek and swift, armed and armored craft of Rum Row off the twelve-mile limit; corruption and scandal dogged politician and policeman alike. Millions drank who never drank before[1]; and alcoholism, which had always been a problem, became practically a national disease—and a national killer(of 480 thousand gallons of booze confiscated in New York in one "dry" year and subjected to chemical analysis 98 percent was found to contain poisons). Teetotalers were seemingly harder to come by. Women not only took up smoking but drinking, and in a big way. Comments one student of the era on the Eighteenth Amendment's intended effect to lock the swinging doors to father: "Actually, during the saloon days at least one saw father's feet . . . after the Eighteenth came in, father disappeared and one no longer saw much of mother either."[2]

According to the same commentator, there were three open saloons in the shadow of police headquarters in Albany, New York, before Prohibition; afterward there were no less than eighteen speakeasies in the area.

---

[1]The Licensed Beverage Industries, Inc. states that 1.95 gallons of liquor were consumed per capita each year during Prohibition; this compares with the pre-Prohibition peak of 1.84 gallons in 1917 and about 1.70 gallons today.
[2]Lee, *op. cit.*, p. 4.

Alva Johnston, a reporter for the *New York Herald Tribune,* told of high school boys in Decatur, Illinois, carrying hip-pocket flasks of whiskey or gin. The Reverend Francis Kasackszul, a Catholic priest, testified in 1926 before a congressional investigating committee that the schoolteachers in his hometown of Sugar Notch, Pennsylvania, "have been complaining about children coming to school under the influence of drink." War between two gangs of student bootleggers at Dartmouth led to the killing of a youth.

Corruption reached practically every law enforcement agency in America. After all, not even a rookie policeman out on his first evening's beat could fail to detect a speakeasy in which men and women walked in straight and sober, many of them to emerge later tipsy and raucous. During the first four dry years, even some one hundred and forty Prohibition agents were jailed. In April 1925, a jury in the federal court in Cincinnati convicted another fifty-eight Prohibition agents and policemen (two Pullman cars were necessary to haul the miscreants to the Atlanta penitentiary) ; and in the same month the Prohibition director for Ohio was found guilty of conspiracy with the underworld.

Violence in America's big cities became rife. It was the era of the gangster and the rumrunner, the bootlegger and the hijacker, the bathtub gin artist and the crooked judge. It was the era of jazz, flappers, flagpole sitters, the coonskin coat, the hip flask, and the jeweled flask for milady's purse. It was the era of big-time gangsterism—of Irving (Waxey Gordon) Wexler, Fandolfo (Frankie Marlow) Civito, Lawrence (Butch)

Crowley, Arthur (Dutch Schultz) Flegenheimer, Charles (Lucky) Luciano, Francesco (Frankie Yale) Uale, Al (Big Shot, also Scarface) Capone, and others too numerous to mention.

Capone, according to the head of the Chicago Crime Commission, spent $260,000 to help put into office Mayor William Hale Thompson (who gained additional notoriety when he publicly threatened to "punch King George in the snoot," and continually dismissed stories of killing and corruption in Chicago, with an airy wave of his hand and an "It's all newspaper talk"). Complained Capone: "I call myself a businessman. I make my money by supplying a popular demand. If I break the law, my customers are as guilty as I am. When I sell liquor, it's bootlegging. When my patrons serve it on silver trays on Lake Shore Drive, it's hospitality."[1]

Just how did America get into such a fix? The process is not too dissimilar to that encountered in any new phase of regulation such as today's vogue for consumerism—the mentality seen in the easy call of "let's pass a law." Congress, which passed the Volstead Act, and the state legislatures, which ratified the Eighteenth Amendment, must of course bear the major responsibility for Prohibition. Yet a lot of the responsibility is also traceable to the dubious but lively art of pressure politics—universal in regulation—and, in the case at hand, to the rise of two powerful lobbies—the Anti-Saloon League, founded in 1893, and the Women's

---

[1]Quoted in Herbert Asbury, *The Great Illusion*, Doubleday, 1950, p. 291.

Christian Temperance Union, founded in 1874. Too, there was a Prohibition party, founded in 1869, but its influence never amounted to much.

The Anti-Saloon League issued literature by the ton. According to its *Year Book,* in 1916 the League, which owned its own printing plant at Westerville, Ohio, was putting out seventeen weekly, biweekly, and monthly editions of the *American Issue,* the organization's official paper, in addition to other periodicals and literally millions of copies of pamphlets, tracts, folders, leaflets, charts, and books. All told, Wayne B. Wheeler, the League's general counsel, admitted to a league outlay of about $35 million to bring about Prohibition.

A major figure in the Anti-Saloon League was Bishop James Cannon, Jr., a Methodist who headed the Virginia Anti-Saloon League when it won a state-wide prohibition law in 1914 and who later became the outspoken chairman of the national league's legislative committee. Perhaps as much as any man, Bishop Cannon defeated Governor Smith's bid for the presidency, though the Bishop was a lifelong Democrat and a delegate to the 1928 Democratic Convention. When Smith balked at running wholeheartedly on the party's Dry plank, Bishop Cannon was galvanized into action. In many Southern states the Dry cleric spoke for Smith's defeat, stressing the governor's Roman Catholicism and lukewarmness to Prohibition. In the end, eight Southern states voted Republican in November 1928, four for the first time since Reconstruction.

The Women's Christian Temperance Union was also heavily in the pamphleteering business and owned its own publishing plant at Evanston, Illinois. In the

Smith-Hoover campaign of 1928, the W.C.T.U. printed
and distributed ten million copies of a leaflet detailing
Alfred E. Smith's voting record as a member of the
New York State Legislature.

A leading light of the Prohibition movement was
hatchet-wielding Carry Nation. She said it was in Medicine Lodge, Kansas, that she received divine appointment to destroy the saloon. Beginning in 1900 she
reinforced her public prayers and condemnations of
Demon Rum with a personal campaign of violence on
saloons; she and her female disciples, armed with
hatchets, swept through the country, smashing whiskey
bottles and beer kegs in what she called "hatcheta-
tions."

Still, once Prohibition got on the books the Drys had
a tough time keeping it there, especially as unforeseen
problem piled upon unforeseen problem. Prohibition by
the mid-twenties had become a national obsession, dom-
inating all other issues. The army of Prohibition's dis-
affected grew. In 1925, Pierre S. Du Pont, once an
ardent Prohibitionist, joined the Association Against the
Prohibition Amendment (A.A.P.A.). By 1929, association board members also included such stalwarts as
Lammot and Irénée Du Pont; General W. W. Atter-
bury, president of the Pennsylvania Railroad; former
Secretary of State Elihu Root; John J. Raskob, chairman of the Democratic National Committee; Haley
Fiske, president of the Metropolitan Life Insurance
Company; Newcomb Carlton, president of Western
Union; and Percy S. Straus, president of R. H. Macy
& Company.

The Anti-Saloon League fought hard against the

A.A.P.A. and all who would tamper with the Volstead
Act or the Eighteenth Amendment. Wavering politi-
cians would meet with the league's swift retribution. As
H. L. Mencken described the league's tactics:[1]

> The Prohibitionist leaders, being mainly men of
> wide experience in playing upon the prejudices
> and emotions of the mob, developed a tech-
> nique of terrorization that was almost irresist-
> ible. The moment a politician ventured to speak
> against them he was accused of the grossest
> baseness. It was whispered that he was a secret
> drunkard and eager to safeguard his tipple; it
> was covertly hinted that he was in the pay of
> the Whiskey Ring, the Beer Trust, or some
> other such bugaboo. The events showed that
> the shoe was actually on the other foot—that
> many of the principal suporters of Prohibition
> were on the payroll of the Anti-Saloon League,
> and that judges, attorneys general and other
> high officers of justice afterward joined them
> there. But the accusations served their purpose.

Yet if the event of war paved the way into Prohibition, the event of depression paved its exit. The Wets,
not exactly displaying altogether sound economic thinking, blamed the Great Depression on the Noble Experiment, arguing, among other things, that Prohibition was
foreclosing hundreds of thousands of jobs—and costing

---

[1]H. L. Mencken, *Notes on Democracy,* Jonathan Cape, 1927,
pp. 141-142.

the federal, state, and local treasuries millions of dollars in fruitless enforcement and lost liquor taxes.

In 1932 both presidential candidates, Roosevelt and Hoover, aided and abetted by still another pressure group, the Women's Organization for National Prohibition Reform (known on the side as the Bacchantian Maidens), called for repeal of the Eighteenth Amendment. In April 1933, beer of not more than 3.2 percent alcoholic content was authorized by Congress and later that year the then requisite thirty-sixth state, Utah, voted for ratification of the congressional resolution calling for repeal of the Eighteenth Amendment. On December 5, 1933, the Twenty-First Amendment became part of the Constitution, and President Roosevelt declared:[1]

> I ask the whole hearted cooperation of all our citizens to the end that this return of individual freedom shall not be accompanied by the repugnant conditions that obtained prior to the adoption of the 18th Amendment and those that have existed since its adoption . . . I ask especially that no State shall by law or otherwise authorize the return of the saloon either in its old form or in some modern guise.

But Prohibition did not die so easily. It lived on in a number of states. (Oklahoma, said one of its most revered philosophers, Will Rogers, would stay Dry as

---

[1]*Public Papers and Addresses of Franklin D. Roosevelt,* Vol. II, Random House, 1938, pp. 511-512.

long as the last voter could stagger to the polls.) And in states voting Wet, negative regulation turned to positive regulation via tax and license gimmicks. Today the free lunch and swinging doors are no more. The saloon is dead all right, but only in name. A whole set of Depression laws and a new breed of architects have come in with cocktail lounges, bars, grills, taverns, inns, parlors, licensed "package stores," and state liquor retailing units. Michigan, apparently concerned about the return of the free lunch, once ruled out pretzels at the bar, and Delaware outlawed stand-up bars. Today licenses are frequently hard to come by (and in some states sell on the open market at sums ranging into the thousands of dollars); inspectors of all kinds flourish; liquor taxes have never been higher (one federal tax alone on whiskey amounts to $10.50 a gallon).

The results of such liquor legislation and taxation have been some of the pitfalls of Prohibition all over again, if on a reduced scale. In 1963, the New York State Liquor Authority, for example, was exposed as a racket-ridden, graft-laden bureaucracy. In a recent year, according to figures released by the Licensed Beverage Industries, Inc., the official voice of the tax-paying liquor industry, federal, state, and local governments seized 18,594 illicit stills and made 18,137 arrests of operators of such stills.

At any rate, Prohibition and its long-lingering aftermath suggest that regulation of any single industry is not easy, that business regulation is indeed people regulation—i.e., consumer regulation. Lawful and "moral" Prohibition produced not the intended "era of clear thinking and clean living" but an era of law-lessness and moral laxness. The "protected" consumer lost again.

The experience of Prohibition seems to reinforce the theory that interventionistic regulation tends to produce circumstances less satisfactory than those the intervention was designed to cure. As Ludwig von Mises described intervention:[1]

> Economics does not say that isolated government interference with the prices of only one commodity or a few commodities is unfair, bad or unfeasible. It says that such interference produces results contrary to its purpose, that it makes conditions worse, not better, from the point of view of the government and those backing its interference.

Thus, taking a cue from the Prohibition experience, from Lord Acton on the corruptibility of power and from Professor Parkinson on the inherent expansibility of bureaucracy, the free society should seek to minimize regulation and maximize the free market. But not everyone agrees, and a debate develops over economic regulation, over the free market versus government intervention, over private decisions versus public controls, over consumer sovereignty versus producer, and now increasingly, government sovereignty in the marketplace—in sum, over consumer regulation versus consumer liberation.

---

[1]Ludwig von Mises, *Human Action,* Yale, 1949, p. 758.

CHAPTER II

The Consumer Movement and the Food and Drug Administration

And it came to pass that to that land of fiery creatures which was called Detroiticus there came an advocate. Of little fame, but of great determination was he. And he spake unto the Council of the Greats saying unto them, "For ye have loosed upon the land a plague of things, and these Things do maim and even kill my brethren, and these Things ye have called Corvairs. Yea, though ye are great and I am humble, I do call upon ye to remove this plague from the land. And this call I make for the Kingdom of Consumers." And the advocate, he called Nader, returned to the capital city where he caused to be written new laws; laws which would aid and comfort his people, the Consumers.

—Roger E. Celler
The Challengers
Public Affairs Council, 1971

The irony of it: On one side of the Rio Grande, the Mexican consumer seeks to keep body and soul together on a per capita income, in terms of GNP, of $546 a year, while his neighbor to the north has $4,121 a year.[1] The United States, with about 6 percent of the world's population and land area, produces and consumes about 40 percent of the Free World's goods and services. The American consumer takes it for granted that American free enterprise will year after year produce more and more new conveniences, new comforts, new designs, new drugs, new gadgets. The American consumer is able to purchase and consume a greater quantity and wider variety of goods and services than anyone else on earth. Drama and music in one's own home. Language and culture from a plastic disc or tape. Travel abroad at the speed of sound. (And other aspects of quality of life.) The wonders of electricity. Time-saving appliances and quickly-prepared meals liberating the American women long before the Women's Liberation movement caught up with the idea. The pampered American consumer, in short, never had it so good.

But, paradoxically, this virtual embarrassment of riches has become a launching pad for, as noted, a new movement called "consumerism." The movement holds

---

[1]U.S. Agency for International Development, Statistics and Reports Division, "Gross National Product—Growth Rates and Trend Data by Region and Country," April 1969. Incidentally, this source gives India's per capita income as $86 a year. All figures are for 1968.

that the consumer is increasingly unable to exercise "informed choices." It holds that the marketplace can no longer be policed by consumer sovereignty and market competition, that therefore government intervention in the marketplace and what amounts to general harassment of industry and commerce have to be the order of the day.

Why? Consumerism looks upon the consumer as largely unprotected and upon the very quantity and variety of available goods and services as complicating choice. Now there are about eight thousand items in a modern supermarket, up from some three thousand in 1950. Consumerism also regards the technological complexity of many consumer products as bewildering to the average consumer, especially in making comparative evaluations of price, safety, and performance.

Accordingly, consumerist leaders such as President Nixon's Special Assistant for Consumer Affairs Virginia Knauer, New York City Commissioner of Consumer Affairs Bess Meyerson, and free-wheeling, free-lance consumerist Ralph Nader are pressing for a wide range of interventionist measures to "protect" the consumer. Many consumer-oriented groups have joined the movement. In Washington and other government centers, consumerist demands tend to be heeded because—be it remembered—consumers vote and corporations don't. Government remembers, and the way it usually remembers is by passing a law and creating a bureaucracy.

Yet while "consumerism" as a word is new, the movement is not. The first wave of consumerism in the United States began in the last decades of the nineteenth century. By then railroads crisscrossed the nation, creating national markets; refrigerated railroad freight cars began to carry meat from the stockyards of Chicago to the butcher shops of the East; and advertisements for trademarked products began to appear in profusion in national magazines. It was, in all, a period of rapid industrialization, growing urbanization, and accelerating change, supposedly rendering the consumer unable to cope in the world of Big Railroads and Big Business.

So, to "protect" the consumer against Big Railroads and Big Business, Congress passed the Interstate Commerce Act in 1887 to deal with the railroads, and the Sherman Antitrust Act in 1890 to deal with the large corporations. This legislation reflected and strengthened the consumerism of the time.

One early organization active in consumerism was the National Consumer League. The league, organized in 1899 by Florence Kelley of Chicago's Hull House, encouraged the purchase of products made under league-approved working conditions. It awarded its label to manufacturers who met certain safety, sanitation, and wage and hours standards.

Other forerunners of today's consumerists were the muckrakers and consumerists of the first decade of this century. To Frank Norris, big business was *The Octopus* (1901) and to Upton Sinclair, the meatpacking industry was *The Jungle* (1906). Largely due to the influence of Sinclair's *Jungle* and to a long and stormy campaign by Dr. Harvey W. Wiley, chief chemist of the U.S. Department of Agriculture and a Ralph Nader of his day, two more landmark consumer laws were passed in Congress. One was the Pure Food and Drug Act of 1906, which prohibited poisonous or other injurious additives to food and drugs, adulterants used to disguise inferior quality and unsanitary manufacturing or processing conditions in food and drug factories. The other landmark consumer law was the Meat Inspection Act of 1907. This act established federal meat inspection and prohibited interstate sales of meat or meat products deemed unfit for human consumption.

Other legislation influenced by early consumerism included the Clayton and Federal Trade Commission Acts of 1914, the Federal Power Commission Act of 1920, and the Prohibition Amendment which became effective in 1920. With these laws on the books and with, incidentally, Republicans in charge of the White House and the Congress, consumerism scored again in 1928, when the Agricultural Appropriation Act established the Food, Drug and Insecticide Administration. The name of the agency was changed to the Food and Drug Administration by the Agricultural Appropriation Act of 1931.

Consumerism also scored on the literary front when *Your Money's Worth* by Stuart Chase and F. J. Schlink was published in 1927 and became a best seller by cataloging alleged failures of a host of new consumer durables. Mr. Schlink followed up this sensation with an even greater sensation, *100,000,000 Guinea Pigs,* coauthored with Arthur Kallet in 1933, a book alleging misleading advertising, and food and cosmetic adulteration and deterioration. The books started Mr. Schlink

on a career as a consumer advocate which he continues
to this day.

A legislative response to this consumerism of another
era was an enlarged Pure Food, Drug and Cosmetic
Act in 1938. The new act expanded previous provisions
and added regulations on cosmetics and therapeutic
devices. The act also provided controls on the introduction of new drugs by requiring permission from the
Food and Drug Administration before a new drug could
be sold in interstate commerce. Applications for new
drugs could be rejected on grounds of inadequate testing or failure to meet standards of efficacy, reliability,
or safety.

Consumerism, more or less dormant for a generation,
accelerated in the decade of the 1960s. It was aided
and abetted as in past waves by a number of social
reform-minded writers. For example, Rachel Carson
warned in her *Silent Spring* (1962) of dangers in the
use of pesticides by food growers. And Vance Packard
in his *Hidden Persuaders* (1957) inveighed against
subtle and supposedly persuasive powers wielded by wily
advertisers over defenseless consumers; he followed up
this work with *The Waste Makers* (1960), a book
charging that, among other things, consumer-goods
producers "planned" the obsolescence of their products
and promoted a "throwaway" spirit among the consuming public.

Once more government listened and responded. On
March 15, 1962, President Kennedy sent a Consumer
Message to Congress maintaining that consumers "are
the only important group in the economy who are not

effectively organized, whose views are often not heard." Accordingly, he proclaimed four "basic" consumer rights:

The right to safety. Products should not harm or damage the user and should perform according to manufacturers' claims.

The right to be informed. Complete and accurate product information should be provided.

The right to choose. Consumer choice should be preserved, based on the right to choose a diverse number of products.

The right to be heard. The consumer viewpoint should be given greater consideration by producers of goods and services.

Soon after this message, President Kennedy formed the Consumer Advisory Council. In 1964, President Johnson added the President's Committee on Consumer Interests with Esther Peterson as chairman. Another plum for the consumerists came shortly afterwards with Mrs. Peterson's designation as Special Assistant to the President for Consumer Affairs. Mrs. Peterson was succeeded by former movie actress Betty Furness; and with the changeover to the Nixon Administration in 1969, Virginia Knauer took charge.

The special assistant to the President for consumer affairs wields considerable power. She heads the President's Committee on Consumer Interests, a group made up of the heads of twelve government consumer-oriented agencies and any others the President may designate. According to its executive mandate, the committee is directed to consider how federal action can be used to help the consumer. Mrs. Knauer also is executive secretary of the Consumer Advisory Council, a group of twelve private citizens appointed by the President to advise the government on consumer interests and problems.

In addition, the President's special assistant works with state groups on proposed state consumer legislation and testifies frequently before Congress on consumer measures under consideration. She deals directly with corporation heads to help solve consumer problems. She is an advocate of a Consumer Register—a popularized version of the *Federal Register* understandable to the layman so that consumers and consumerists can be alerted to proposed federal regulations in the consumer field.

Naturally, like his two predecessors, President Nixon is apparently imbued with some of the fervor of consumerism. In late 1969, in tones reminiscent of President Kennedy, President Nixon proclaimed a "Buyer's Bill of Rights" in his Consumer Message:

> I believe that the buyer in America today has the right to make an intelligent choice among products and services.
>
> The buyer has the right to accurate information on which to make his free choice.
>
> The buyer has the right to expect that his health and safety is taken into account by those who seek his patronage.

The buyer has the right to register his dissatisfaction, and have his complaint heard and weighed, when his interests are badly served.

Besides the executive branch response to consumerist pressure in the 1960s, the legislative branch responded with an outpouring of laws designed to protect the consumer in one way or another from unsafe or unhealthy products. With Ralph Nader's appearance on the Washington scene in the mid-sixties, the safety side of consumerist legislation went into high gear. Consumerist legislation for the decade includes:

The Color Additive Amendments to the Food, Drug and Cosmetic Act in 1960, and further amendments in 1962.

The Hazardous Substances Labeling Act of 1960.

The National Traffic and Motor Vehicle Safety Act of 1966.

The Radiation Control for Health and Safety Act of 1968.

The National Gas Pipeline Safety Act of 1968.

The Wholesale Poultry Act of 1968.

The Wholesale Meat Act of 1969.

The Child Protection and Safety Toy Act of 1969.

Not only did Congress consider the consumer's health and safety, it considered his desire, as expressed by consumerists, for more information. Thus two sweeping acts were passed. First came the Fair Packaging and Labeling Act of 1966 and its amendment in 1968. Also known as the Hart Act after its sponsor, Senator Philip Hart of Michigan, the act requires identification of commodity and manufacturer plus information as to contents and net quantity. The act also gives the Food and Drug Administration and the Federal Trade Commission certain discretionary powers "to prevent the deception of consumers or to facilitate price comparisons as to any consumer commodity." Discretionary provisions are concerned with labeling of ingredients, number of servings, descriptions of size, and cents-off labeling.

Next came the Truth in Lending Act of 1969. The act requires disclosure of all costs of borrowing, and is especially aimed at installment loans. The act requires that lenders inform borrowers of annual rates of interest and costs in dollars of any loan as well as charges for appraisals, credit reports, finder's fees, and service charges. Consumerism in the public-sector also includes the consumer laws of some thirty-five states so far. Still, concern for the consumer is anything but the sole preserve of the public sector. The private sector has produced a number of consumer allies: voluntary industry-wide codes, private testing groups, business self-regulating organizations, the individual or organization consumer crusader and, of course, the greatest consumer ally of all, the free market, as discussed in Chapter I.

Examples of voluntary industry-wide codes are found in the television and motion picture industries. While debatable as to content and for a long while open to charges of censorship, the film code offers at least labels on movies as to audience suitability. In the code of the Motion Picture Association of America, movies are labeled on suitability for various audiences from "G" for general audiences to "X" for "under 17 not admitted." The code dates back to the Hays Office of the 1930s. Then a Hays-condemned rating could be box office poison; today an "X" rating, the "condemned" equivalent of the Hays days, is as likely as not to spell box office success.

The TV Code of the National Association of Broadcasters set limits on the number and length of commercials in given time periods, prohibits commercials on such things as astrology, hard liquor, mind reading and race track tip sheets, and sets standards for program content—as does the Federal Communications Commission (covered in Chapter VIII).

Business self-regulation through private organizations is also evidenced by many trade associations and by Better Business Bureaus run by local businessmen in one hundred forty cities throughout the country. Dating back to 1912, the bureaus' activities include the investigation of consumer complaints against false charities, so-called "fire" and going-out-of-business sales, and deceptive direct-mail and door-to-door selling. In 1969 the Better Business Bureau of New York ran consumer education seminars in Harlem on the topic, "What You Show Know About Buying." Indeed, the Council of Better Business Bureaus, an independent, national co-

ordinating organization of local bureaus, has been newly
launched to add muscle to consumer complaints. Now,
for example, the motorist who buys a lemon has a national as well as local ombudsman to carry his case to
the highest echelons of corporate management. Moreover, the council seeks also to become a national consumer information resource center, gathering and
disseminating statistical and other consumer information. The information should further enhance consumer
education and producer adaptation. As H. Bruce Pal-
mer, the council's president, put it in a 1971 speech:

> The council intends to close the gap between
> what people expect of business and what busi-
> ness promises. This means that we will help
> business speak in language that consumers un-
> derstand—with full and *honest* disclosure. At
> the same time, we intend to help people better
> understand relative values, product-life expec-
> tancy, the cost of credit, how to find real bar-
> gains—and how to select what they need and
> want—letting people attach their own personal
> set of values and either *buy*—or *pass* it by.

Business self-regulation also includes the use of direct
"hot line" telephone communications between consumer and producer—in the case of Whirlpool, toll-free calls
from anywhere in the U.S. to Benton Harbor, Michigan, site of Whirlpool's main office. Similarly, the Association of Home Appliance Manufacturers, the Gas
Appliance Manufacturers Association and the American Retail Federation established the Major Appliance
Consumer Action Panel to act as an independent court

of last resort for unresolved consumer complaints. The eight panel members are chosen from outside the industry and, with the exception of travel expenses, are not paid for their work. Again, a 50-member National Advertising Review Board, sponsored by three advertising industry trade groups and the Council of Better Business Bureaus, handles complaints about false and deceptive advertising. A statement describing the board's activities declares that if the board decides an ad is misleading but can't persuade the advertiser to change it, "the matter will be turned over to the Federal Trade Commission or other appropriate government agency, and the board's findings will be publicized."

Independent testing groups are also among the private aids to the consumer. For example, Underwriters Laboratories, founded by the National Board of Fire Underwriters in 1894, tests electrical safety features of virtually all electrical appliances sold today. Testing is financed by fees charged manufacturers for running tests and for certifying safety with the UL Seal of Approval.

Other "Seals of Approval" are given by *Good Housekeeping* and *Parents* magazines. Both magazines certify that any claim made in advertisements for products advertised in the magazines and awarded "seals" are factual. Both magazines guarantee that if any advertised product or service turns out to be defective, refunds or replacements will be given. To be sure, the "seals" work two ways: The magazines use them as selling inducements to gain advertising space, and the consumer can use them as guides to purchases.

Consumers' Research, the original independent non-

profit organization devoted solely to testing and reporting to the public on a broad range of consumer goods,
was started in 1928. Its founder, F. J. Schlink, is the
aforementioned co-author of *Your Money's Worth* and
100,000,000 Guinea Pigs. Consumers' Research is still
performing testing services in its Washington, New
Jersey, laboratories and reporting evaluations of products in its monthly *Consumer Bulletin* magazine.

In 1935, Consumers Union of Mount Vernon, New
York, was formed by a group of union-minded Consumers' Research employees, who left the Schlink
organization after failing to organize Consumers' Research. Colston Warne, the president of Consumers
Union, now heads a staff of three hundred, including
fifty engineers, who test and publish results of their
tests in *Consumer Reports* magazine, which has a cir-
culation of around two million a month.

To insure independence and credibility, neither
Consumers' Research nor Consumers Union accepts advertising from manufacturers nor allows them to use
ratings to advertise products. Both organizations play
the role of consumer and purchase products anony-
mously in representative retail stores. They then test
these products for durability, comfort, performance,
economy, and safety, among other things. Accordingly,
over the years Consumers' Research and Consumers
Union have reported on which dishwasher detergent
washes dishes cleanest, which refrigerators have the
most efficient storage design, which automobiles are
safest and most economical, and so on for literally
thousands of products.

The consumer crusaders, both individual and organizational, can augment the market by calling attention to environmental and product deficiencies and by otherwise educating the public. But they can also sometimes hamper the market when they shift from advocating benign regulation to advocating interventionistic regulation. Uncrowned king of the crusaders is Ralph Nader. Like earlier crusaders such as Upton Sinclair and Frank Norris, Nader helped make his name a household word with a book. His *Unsafe at Any Speed* (1965) propelled Congress and the auto industry into a super-safety campaign. Today Nader and his "Raiders," usually volunteer college and law school students, investigate just about everything from nursing homes to the First National City Bank of New York.

Another consumerist crusader is John F. Banzhaf III, who, like Nader, is a young lawyer. With the aid of the FCC, Banzhaf fought for and won free time on TV and radio stations for antismoking commercials. Now, all TV and radio commercials for cigarettes have been banned, as of January 2, 1971. Again, like Nader, Banzhaf has disciples. His are "Banzhaf's Bandits" and they investigate, among other things, collection agency practices.

Besides the individual consumerist there is the consumerist organization. The largest is the Consumer Federation of America. It includes some one hundred fifty groups in its membership, most of them cooperatives, and some political action groups such as the American Public Power Association, American Public Gas Association, and the Tennessee Valley Public Power Association. The federation advises its members which consumer issues to publicize, which members of Congress and congressional bills to promote or oppose, when to testify, and when to communicate with members of Congress.

After this outline of consumerism and consumerists, of public and private protectors of the consumer, the question still remains: Does the consumer benefit from consumerism? The answer depends on the degree and quality of consumerism. Establishment of reasonable standards and improvement of the workings of the market can be benign and most welcome regulation; but much, if not most, current consumerism appears to be of the interventionistic type. Indeed, most consumerists seem unaware of the cleansing and consumer-protecting nature of the market.

The regulatory agency tailored from its beginning to meet consumer demands most directly is the Food and Drug Administration. Clearly, the Food and Drug Administration is on the side of the angels in seeking that drugs be safe and efficacious, that cosmetics be harmless, that foods be pure, safe and wholesome, and that all these items be factually labeled.

This is a tall order. With a budget under $100 million, the FDA regulates the $150 billion food, drug, and cosmetic industries. It administers, among many other programs, the shellfish and milk sanitation programs. It soon may be saddled with enforcement of new legislation on therapeutic devices. It employs approximately five thousand people—food inspectors, laboratory technicians, industrial engineers and cadres of white-collar workers. It is administered by a commissioner under the direction of HEW's assistant secretary for health and scientific affairs. It is headquartered in Rockville, Maryland, not far from Washington. It has twenty-seven district and regional offices to carry out field enforcement of the several laws under its jurisdiction.

The FDA has three bureaus—the Bureau of Foods, Pesticides and Product Safety, the Bureau of Drugs, and the Bureau of Veterinary Medicine. Its Office of the Hearing Examiner conducts prehearing conferences and administrative hearings of an adjudicative and rule-making nature. The rules relate to standards for foods, food additives, drugs, cosmetics, pesticides, and other potentially harmful products. After hearings, the examiner evaluates the evidence, prepares reports, makes tentative findings and recommendations for use by the commissioner in making a final agency decision— for example, whether or not a particular new drug is approved for commercial use, or whether or not a food additive such as cyclamate should be removed from the FDA's "Generally Recognized As Safe" (GRAS) list of some seven hundred food additives. So, directly and indirectly, the FDA's staff and a battery of laws and regulations touches virtually every American consumer every day.

Understandably, then, the FDA gets embroiled with the industries it regulates. The food, drug and cosmetic industries have the well-funded efforts of their trade associations and Washington law firms to oversee the FDA. In the drug area, for example, some physicians have questioned the propriety of FDA Commissioner Charles C. Edward's proposed requirement that a statement describing the risks of oral contraceptives be included in every package going to users. The Pharmaceutical Manufacturers Association has claimed FDA's proposed rules on proof of effectiveness of drugs are unrealistic and illegal. And the Council for Senior Citizens and the American Public Health Association have sued the commissioner to force faster withdrawal of drugs from the market which are deemed ineffective by review panels of the National Academy of Sciences.

Well, then, just how effective has the FDA been? Since 1955, the agency has been the object of fourteen major critical studies by citizen and government task forces and of numerous critical congressional hearings. The criticism has been sharp. The 1969 *Kinslow Report* on the FDA concluded that the agency was largely ineffectual in protecting consumers, mainly due to congressional failure to provide enough "legislation, manpower, and money." But the Kinslow Report was the product of the FDA's own Baltimore District Director, Maurice D. Kinslow, who has since been promoted to acting assistant commissioner.

Another 1969 report on the FDA, this one by HEW Secretary Robert Finch's own FDA review committee headed by Deputy Undersecretary Frederic V. Malek, also scored the FDA but laid the blame on internal organizational problems and incompetence within the FDA. Turnover at the top has accordingly been high at the FDA, with three commissioners in the last five years.

Whether due to incompetence or organizational problems or some other reason, the FDA has had more than its share of agency failures. In the case of cyclamates, for example, the FDA was apparently most complacent in the face of long-mounting evidence against the use of this particular food additive. Only as late as 1969 did the government act when HEW Secretary Robert Finch announced: "I am today ordering that the artificial sweetener, cyclamate, be removed from the list of substances generally recognized as safe for use in foods." Yet as early as 1950 the FDA itself had noted malignant tumors in laboratory rats after they were subjected to cyclamates. In addition, in 1954 the government was warned by the Food Nutrition Board of the National Academy of Sciences-National Research Council that cyclamates were potentially harmful. There were other warnings. But for one reason or another the FDA could not bring itself to act until 1969.

The FDA, however, is not always so lethargic. At times it can move with vigor, particularly against what it regards as medical quackery and food faddism. For example, the FDA obtained an injunction in 1956 against Dr. Wilhelm Reich, an avant-garde Viennese psychoanalyst, well known for his theories on sexuality and the author of a psychiatric work, *Character Analysis.*

What bothered the FDA about Dr. Reich was that the psychiatrist apparently claimed he had found a cure for cancer. He also was selling devices called orgone boxes which he claimed could improve the health of the user. The FDA believed the orgone boxes came under the Food, Drug and Cosmetic Act inclusion of medical devices, and therefore moved against Dr. Reich. But the devices were not the only target of the FDA—Dr. Reich's writings were also targets. Interpreting the Act to construe the Reich books as directions and inspirations for the use of the devices, the FDA got a court injunction not only to bar the devices from interstate commerce and prohibit the sale of Reich's works, but to destroy "all documents, bulletins, pamphlets, journals and booklets" of Reich's research foundation. In compliance with the injunction, an FDA inspector went to Dr. Reich's office in July 1956 and, in the psychiatrist's presence, burned his books. According to the FDA inspector, Dr. Reich was most pleasant and said that "his books had been burnt in Germany, and he did not think it would ever happen again, but here they were being burned once again."[1] Dr. Reich refused to obey the injunction and wound up in a federal penitentiary where he died after seventeen months.

Even the thalidomide ban, for which the FDA takes credit, has adverse bureaucratic implications for the agency. Dr. Frances Kelsey, a then recently hired FDA medical official, got the job of evaluating the Robert S. Merrell Company's new drug application for thalidomide in 1960. Dr. Kelsey became a friend of Dr. Barbara Moulton, who had resigned as a medical official at FDA in protest over what she claimed was the FDA's careless regulation of drugs. At the Kefauver drug hearings in 1960, Dr. Moulton scored FDA's lax drug control policies as causing "people . . . to be injured and even to die."[2]

---

[1]James S. Turner, *The Chemical Feast: Ralph Nader's Study Group Report on the Food and Drug Administration,* Grossman, 1970, p. 35.
[2]Turner, *op. cit.,* p. 227.

In 1961 Dr. Kelsey, who was present at the Moulton testimony, discovered in the *British Medical Journal* that thalidomide was associated with peripheral neuritis. Later in 1961 the U.S. Ambassador to Germany sent a dispatch to the State Department that some one hundred birth defects in Germany had been traced to thalidomide. But the FDA top command did not inform Dr. Kelsey of the dispatch, nor did they have the Merrell Company cancel its testing program. In December 1961 Merrell notified 137 doctors distributing the pills on a test basis not to give them to women of childbearing age. In April 1962 Dr. Kelsey sought from Merrell a more complete list of doctors dispensing thalidomide. She received a sharply expanded list of 1,070 names. In May 1962 she supplied the FDA with a memorandum spelling out the thalidomide risk.

Still the FDA did not move. In July 1962 the *Washington Post* broke the story, and Commissioner Larrick at last dispatched FDA inspectors around the country to recall all thalidomide pills. In August 1962 President Kennedy asked all Americans to remove unlabeled pills from their medicine cabinets. Later he publicly commended Dr. Kelsey for her role in the thalidomide story.

In any event, delay seems endemic to FDA procedures. This delay is not without benefit—or cost. The benefit lies in possible lives saved or not harmed by the FDA's lengthy testing and paperwork requirements. The cost lies in higher prices for drugs due to the time lag between discovery in the laboratory and availability in the drugstore. The cost also lies in the possibility of lives lost or harmed through not having faster use of new drugs, a delay caused by a prolonged testing stage.

Most drug firms do extensive testing themselves—for their own self-interest—before any drug is marketed. Should a harmful or defective drug be sold and cause harm or death, the guilty firm could be sued for heavy damages, as they can be even on FDA-approved drugs. The risk of costly suits and of damage to reputation is so great as to virtually preclude all but the most irresponsible firms from purposely marketing harmful or misrepresented drugs.

Well, where does the FDA go from here? The "here" is none too good, as knowledgeable people in and out of FDA have long been saying: Ralph Nader, for example, in his introduction to James Turner's *The Chemical Feast* (1970), a study of the FDA, says that the FDA has been negligent in blocking what he alleges is a decline in the nutritional adequacy of American diets. Because the FDA "has so shirked its duties," he writes, that American food companies "have transformed the defrauding of consumers into a competitive advantage."[1]

But neither Mr. Nader nor his raiders seek to get at the heart of the problem—namely interventionistic regulation itself.

Conceivably the FDA could be but a case of benign regulation—simply setting standards for safe foods and drugs. But in practice the agency has bogged down in red tape and time-consuming bureaucracy and has frequently become a vehicle for intervention and industry

---

[1]Turner, *op. cit.*, pp. x, xi.

harassment by consumerists in and out of government. Further, the agency naturally is a target for politicians seeking headlines and scapegoats and for industry figures seeking privileges and protection. What to do?

A solution may be found through cost-benefit analysis, and on this basis the costs of FDA, as it is presently constituted, may outweigh the benefits. Accordingly, the solution may be to de-politicize and de-governmentalize the FDA as was partly done in the case of the Post Office. In other words, the FDA could become a quasi-official or quasi-private agency such as the U.S. Postal Service, Tennessee Valley Authority, the Federal National Mortgage Association, and the National Academy of Sciences. Or, conceivably the National Academy of Sciences could itself assume the testing, inspection, and safety certification functions of the FDA, with the courts taking over the policing functions. Or, the FDA could even be completely privatized and become analogous to Underwriters Laboratories, funded by the food, drug, pesticide, and cosmetic industries, conducting tests on safety and efficacy and certifying results for the benefit of both consumers and producers, with, again, the courts doing the policing. Whatever is done, the idea for the FDA is to greatly reduce the influence of politics, interventionism, and bureaucracy and the dependency for funds and functions on undependable sources from Congress to the Bureau of the Budget.

Beyond the FDA, cost-benefit analysis may also be helpful in solving the general question of how much testing or other precautionary measures should be undertaken for the consumer. This method of comparing costs of regulation with benefits derived may also be used to evaluate the full range of direct and indirect consumer legislation. Attempting to legislate 100 percent safety, for example, could mean producing automobiles with tank-like characteristics and appliances with very expensive safeguards to withstand practically all forms of misuse. *Reductio ad absurdum,* it could even mean prohibiting practically all drugs, since few if any drugs are 100 percent safe for all people under all circumstances.

Again, quality control and safety features are costly. Thus to require super-performance and super-safety by legislation would price many products out of the consumer's reach and cost the consumer some freedom to choose less quality for less money. Clearly, such costs would be too high, and overall consumer welfare would suffer.

Safety legislation can also be misleading on accident causation. Federal auto safety legislation, for one instance, has the laudable aim of cutting deaths and injury on the highway. Yet it hardly deals with the major factor in all accidents—bad driving. According to the National Safety Council's 1967 statistics, nearly 94 percent of auto accidents were caused by driver failure—speeding, following too closely, turning into the wrong lane, crossing the middle line in the wrong direction, etc. And at least half of all fatal accidents in 1967 involved drunken driving. Further, the council notes that safety belts, made mandatory by federal legislation in 1966 in all new cars, were used only about 40 percent of the time

These data suggest that the driver, even more than the automobile, may be the most productive object of safety efforts. They also suggest that government, apart from establishing reasonable auto-safety standards, can best promote safety by strict enforcement of traffic laws and inspection of motor vehicles. States can also make licensing of drivers more discriminating and penalties for traffic-law infractions more stringent.

But, it will be asked, who will protect the consumer in the absence of his official protectors such as FDA as we know it today? It is a fundamental thesis of this book that the market is not only overwhelmingly the consumer's greatest protector but the very means by which he has attained his affluence and freedom of choice. Still, the market will not operate in a governmental vacuum; it needs government to, among other things, enforce contracts and administer justice. Such administration includes prohibitions against fraud, misrepresentation and negligence. What, then, of proposed laws enabling consumers to bring "class action" suits?

Proposed class action legislation would permit consumers to pool claims too small to warrant individual suits into single suits on behalf of groups of consumers allegedly injured by fraudulent or deceptive business practices. But much depends on legislative intent, on how the legislation is drafted, and on what constructive reforms are achieved for the American judicial system (these reforms are discussed briefly in the final chapter).

On the surface, class action legislation would appear to be a relief act for consumers stung by bad bargains.

But in practice, especially if loosely drawn, it could work out to be an invitation to "legal blackmail" in the words of Caspar Weinberger, former FTC chairman. In other words, we could witness legal harassment of large corporations and a relief act for lawyers scrambling to line up consumers to sue the bigger, more affluent producers considered best able to pay large settlements. Fly-by-night operators, often responsible for the more flagrant abuses of consumers, could be hard to pin down for suits and even harder to make financially able to pay for damages. In such cases, the consumer could probably still be stung on occasion or end up paying prices high enough to reflect heavy corporate contingent liability and litigation costs, although here and there a corporate wrongdoer might be brought to heel. Thus, again, depending on how it is written, consumer class action legislation could wind up as but another dose of interventionistic regulation.

Yet properly drafted to preclude excessive attorneys' fees, the subsidization of "ambulance-chasing" attorneys, and the harassment of business through false or frivolous claims, class-action legislation could be a step forward for the consumer. Proper drafting could include provisions of power to the courts to dismiss nuisance suits or settle claims before trials, and limitations on suits to cases where direct injury is ascertainable. In addition, to discourage interminable open-ended litigation, specified and limited time periods should be set after which, provided notice is duly given, no new plaintiffs will be added to a class action. With such provisions class-action legislation could bring about equity when producers actually practice genuine fraud or deception on consumers. Perhaps, more importantly, it could serve to reinforce the self-disciplining and self-regulating nature of the market, going far toward eliminating what relatively little negligence, fraud and deception exist today.

What of unit pricing? Proposed unit pricing legislation could conceivably provide relief for those consumers hard put to determine whether, for example, the "large," "giant," or "economy" size package is their best buy. Prices by weight, volume, or some other standardized measure stamped on packages or posted conveniently nearby—although adding somewhat to retail costs likely to be passed on to the consumer—could help the consumer decide more easily on his most economical alternative in the marketplace. Caution is still necessary in applying this idea. Individual retailers and states —not the federal government—should perhaps consider unit pricing on an experimental basis. At least at the outset, it should not be applied by decree, but rather by administrative encouragement to voluntary compliance. In other words, the market should be used first to determine the efficacy of the idea. Indeed, in many areas of the country it is now being tried.

The market is still the key, intervention the problem. For all the attention to consumerism, Hendrik S. Houthakker of President Nixon's Council of Economic Advisers put it well when he noted in 1970 that "too much energy still goes into worthy but comparatively minor causes such as the prevention of deceptive practices." Mr. Houthakker wanted to see the consumer movement directed more toward areas of government intervention such as tariff protection and the regulated industries. Here, he said, government and industry already play too large a part, pointing out that "even were government intervention started with the best of intentions, it does not take long before producer pressures take over."

Now, credibility of business is under a consumerist cloud, and a growing segment of the public continues to support sweeping consumer protection laws. But as James M. Roche, chairman of General Motors, said:[1]

> Individuals and agencies have competed—sometimes blindly—to be on the crest of the wave of consumer protection. In the 1960's, consumer legislation came into political vogue. Much of this was necessary, and serves our society well. Yet the short-term political advantage offered by spectacular but unsound consumer legislation can do lasting damage to the very consumers it purports to help.

> The consumer is the loser when irresponsible criticism and ill-conceived legislation break down faith in our economic system, when harassment distracts us from our modern challenges, when the very idea of free enterprise is diminished in the eyes of the young people who must one day manage our businesses.

Mr. Roche's reaction against current consumer legislation ties in with the reaction of Virginia Knauer,

[1]*New York Times,* April 21, 1971.

President Nixon's consumer adviser, who discovered, after a two-year study, at least three hundred federal consumer programs. The duplication and overlapping made it practically impossible to produce an exact number. For example, she found that the Truth in Lending Program is supervised by the Federal Trade Commission, the Federal Reserve Board, the Agriculture Department, the Federal Deposit Insurance Corporation, the Federal Home Loan Bank Board, the Bureau of Federal Credit Unions, the Comptroller of the Currency, the Interstate Commerce Commission and the Civil Aeronautics Board. She declared: "I just couldn't believe so many people had their fingers in it. It creates a bureaucratic mare's nest. I'm not saying this one is. But the potential is there."[1]

In sum, business must do its part to rebuild its image with the consumer and reaffirm its crucial role in the marketplace. Corporate codes of consumer relations, for example, might go far in improving buyer-seller rapport. So would simplified and modernized warranties and wider use of consumer-producer "hot lines." In these and other ways, the business sector could help coordinate and reinforce the consumer-retailer-producer communication, distribution, and adjudication system, turning the American consumer into a champion of free enterprise.

---

[1]*Wall Street Journal,* April 27, 1971.

CHAPTER III

Competition and
the Antitrust Division

The doctrine of regulation and legislation by "master minds," in whose judgment and will all the people may gladly and quietly acquiesce, has been too glaringly apparent in Washington during these last ten years. Were it possible to find "master minds" so unselfish, so willing to decide unhesitatingly against their own personal interests or private prejudices, men almost god-like in their ability to hold the scales of justice with an even hand, such a government might be to the interest of the country, but there are none such on our political horizon, and we cannot expect a complete reversal of all the teachings of history.

—Franklin D. Roosevelt, 1930

Nineteen seventy was the eightieth anniversary of U.S. antimonopoly policy, and Senator John Sherman

of Ohio, who started it all somewhat innocently with
the Sherman Antitrust Act of 1890, must have turned
over in his grave. This consumeristic policy, which at its
outset was largely a political maneuver—something of a
perfunctory gesture to mollify Populist antibusiness fe-
ver and expedite passage of the Sherman Silver Purchase Act and the McKinley Tariff—has grown from
the simple, straightforward, and worthwhile prohibitions of the Sherman law into a gaggle of modern but
quite enigmatic antitrust criteria—"conscious parallel-
ism," "conglomerate power," "quantitative substantial-
ity," "incipient incipiency," "administered prices,"
"vertical integration," "marketing reciprocity," "resid-
ual polypoly," "atomistic heteropoly," and so on and on
in a dizzying pattern of generally fuzzy, discretionary,
and, above all, contradictory administrative law.

Antitrust regulation, as currently applied, is quite
contradictory. Increasingly it protects not competition
but competitors, not consumers but producers. Antitrust
regulation in other words, is like Janus; it faces two
ways, pro-competition and, strangely, anti-competition.
At times it seeks to promote "hard" open competition
and at other times it favors "soft" closed competition—
competition protective of the "weak" industry or the
"small" business. In fact, Chairman Paul Rand Dixon
of the Federal Trade Commission himself appeared as
a Janus in the very same interview, in almost the same
breath:[1]

---

[1]*U.S. News and World Report,* July 17, 1961, p. 65.
[2]*Brown Shoe Co.* vs. *U.S.,* 370 U.S. 294 (1962).

If [businessmen] like freedom and don't want outright control, then they've got to stand up and be good citizens. They've got to quit their infernal conforming and doing business the easy way. They're going to have to, we might say, expose themselves to the rigors of competition. . . .

We must hold open opportunities for a man with an idea so that, with a little capital, he can go into business and have a fair chance, by his ingenuity, to grow and become big himself. This is very difficult, if you subscribe to what is called "hard" competition. Competition of this kind is war in a jungle, where only the big man can survive.

Another antitrust Janus was Chief Justice Earl Warren who upheld hard competition in one paragraph of a court decision and soft competition in another:[2]

Of course, some of the results of large integrated or chain operations are beneficial to consumers. Their expansion is not rendered unlawful by the mere fact that small independent stores may be adversely affected. It is competition, not competitors, which the Act protects.

But we cannot fail to recognize Congress' desire to promote competition through the protection of viable, small, locally-owned businesses. Con-

gress appreciated that occasional higher costs
and prices might result from the maintenance
of fragmented industries and markets. It re-
solved these competing considerations in favor
of decentralization. We must give effect to that
decision.

Antitrust regulation—to make a rather woolly situation even woolier—is dichotomous. The Antitrust Division of the United States Department of Justice shares
power with the Federal Trade Commission. They obtain power from the aforementioned Sherman Act of
1890, which outlawed conspiracies in restraint of trade;
the Clayton Act of 1914, which illegalized trade practices (including those mergers which presumably lessen
competition and thus are, supposedly, instruments of
monopoly); the Robinson-Patman Act of 1936, a "night-
mare" of legal entanglement according to Professor
Milton Handler of the Columbia Law School, an act
which outlaws price "discrimination" (when not based
on actual cost savings to the producer), a statute designed to protect small businessmen, especially retailers;
and the Celler-Kefauver Antimerger Act of 1950, which
reinforced the antimerger provisions of the Clayton Act.
The FTC gets its birthright in the Federal Trade
Commission Act of 1914, a law setting up and calling
on the commission to keep American competition both
"free and fair"—a dual standard that, in practice, works
out to be quite contradictory and of questionable fairness to the efficient and aggressive competitor and
particularly to the consumer lost in the antitrust

squeeze of legislators, regulators, regulatees, litigants and lobbyists.

Thus antitrust turns out to be a world where the golden rule is competition, but—unlike *the* golden rule— the government does not do unto itself as it does unto others. For others, the rule is to compete—compete as the government defines competition—but the government itself does not practice what it preaches. Whatever businesses the government operates such as the Postal Service or whatever industries or markets it chooses to exempt need not compete, or at least not compete in the commonly understood sense of the word. This is especially seen in the regulated industries—railroads and airlines, for instance—which are hamstrung by their regulators from fully competing, especially in pricing, for fear that some less able competitors might get hurt. Yet the very idea of competition is to achieve division of labor, eliminate the inefficient and promote industrial efficiency, with the result of a national profit of more and better goods for more people at less cost.

So, competition, anyone? Well, some, but never too much. For example, the Clayton Act exempts farm and labor organizations from antitrust jurisdiction—organizations not exactly devoid of political power, and yet sellers of labor services in the case of unions and sellers of agricultural products in the case of farm cooperatives. These sellers—unions and now the whole government-controlled farm sector—have the makings of giant cartels with all the problems of government-induced and protected monopolies. The process of government cartelization can be seen, too, in official United States

participation in the International Sugar Agreement and
the International Coffee Agreement, among other international commodity agreements, in which the government makes sure Americans pay cartel prices for the
coffee they drink and the sugar they eat, and in the
process injures efficient international producers and
world competition. So when the government talks about
the evils of price fixing, it might be well to consider the
words of President Nixon's Office of Management and
Budget head George P. Shultz, then economist and dean
of the University of Chicago graduate business school,
who said in 1965 that the U.S. government is "the
greatest price fixer of all time," from postage stamps to
natural gas, from minimum wages to maximum interest
rates.

Even so, much is made of the executives of General
Electric, Westinghouse, and other electrical manufacturers who were convicted and sent to jail in the winter
of 1960–1961 for overt and collusive price fixing of such
items as transformers, cut-outs, meters, insulators, and
circuit breakers. No doubt about it, the electrical conspiracy was rank—secret meetings under code names,
under different phases of the moon, in private rooms of
swank hotels, in far-away hunting lodges, with the
pockets of the conspirators bulging with coins for long-
distance calls made from public and hence presumably
untapped phones, and the drawing of numbers from a
hat to allocate the rotation of winning bids in a mock
competition staged to hoodwink the supposedly naive
electrical equipment buyers.

This make-believe, which reduced competition to a

lottery, inspired some fine rhetoric from politicians and other public defenders. Attorney General Robert Kennedy, for example, was moved to compare the price-fixing businessmen with the racketeers who manipulate crooked gambling syndicates. Judge J. Cullen Ganey of the federal court in Philadelphia, who had the job of passing sentence, rightfully ripped into the defendant corporations and executives as saboteurs of the free enterprise system and the American consumer.

But not long after the defendant executives had served their time in a federal penitentiary, the Justice Department presented a draft of a consent decree to General Electric and other major electrical equipment producers in which the companies were asked to agree not to charge "unreasonably low prices" on those products where there is a "reasonable probability" that the effect "may be substantially to injure competition or tend to create a monopoly." Translation of this latter phrase: Tend to put a weaker, less efficient and probably much smaller competitor out of business.

So, had General Electric consented to the decree, it would have found itself in the dilemma of having to chart a hazardous course between the Charybdis of unreasonably high prices and the Scylla of unreasonably low prices. Further, the Justice Department had furnished no standard for "reasonable probability" nor any for "unreasonably low prices." Had GE signed the consent decree, it might easily have discovered that today's reasonably low price might be tomorrow's *un*reasonably low price—a price that broke the back of some marginal competitor.

In fact, it is conceivable that executives of the big equipment manufacturers might at least have been partly moved to enter the conspiracy in the first place so as not to eliminate marginal competitors; thus, antitrust could yield the strange fruit of conspiratorial meetings precisely to keep a price umbrella over weak firms whose untimely demise might trigger antitrust forays on industry "concentration." For Washington is very conscious of the number of competitors in each industry, based on the theory that competition is a function of numbers—the greater the number, supposedly the greater the competition. And in pricing matters, Washington often frowns on prices it deems too high, too low, identical, different, discriminatory, administered, or inflationary.

So the world of antitrust is a world where competition is golden, or mostly golden, but "too much" competition is possibly indictable as "predatory," and "too little" competition is equally indictable as "monopolistic." It is a world in which former TVA Chairman David E. Lilienthal seems pressed to the conclusion: "For the antitrust agencies of the Government to seek to punish the successful competitor—acts of coercion or collusion aside—in the name of competition is difficult for me to comprehend."[1] It is a world where, should a number of businessmen get together to allocate markets or fix prices, the businessmen can wind up in jail. But when public or labor officials do the very same thing, as indeed they do, in cotton and wheat, for example,

---

[1]*Big Business: A New Era,* Harper & Row, 1953, p. 175.

and in virtually every organized labor market, their actions are considered praiseworthy, in the best of the liberal tradition.

In this never-never world, ordinary business transactions and practices are increasingly under an antitrust pale, so that antitrust, in the words of antitrust specialist Jesse W. Markham of Harvard University in his May-June 1963 *Harvard Business Review* article, has now been

> extended to those business transactions that corporate executives engage in all the time as ordinary events of industrial and commercial life. It therefore imposes on the decision-making process of business a new and significant constraint. Further, the mounting volume of antitrust actions against business each year is persuasive evidence that the magnitude and dimensions of this constraint have not yet been recognized by those who exercise important decision-making functions.

Thus, many ordinarily law-abiding businessmen frequently do not know if their policies are legal or not until they hear from the FTC, the Antitrust Division, or the courts. This is not to say, however, that businessmen are innocents in the antitrust story, as the electrical conspiracy case proved. One of the ironies of American business life is the endless public relations homage paid to competition, especially in after-dinner speeches and business conventions, as a fine and glorious institution akin in stature to motherhood and the home—while an endless search goes on to somehow escape from competition. As Adam Smith sagely noted:[1]

> People of the same trade seldom meet together,
> even for merriment and diversion, but the con-
> versation ends in a conspiracy against the pub-
> lic, or in some contrivance to raise prices.

Smith certainly had a point, and antitrust enthusiasts seldom tire of quoting him, but they don't generally quote the rest of the passage, for Smith also noted that, with freedom of entry, combinations in restraint of trade would have a strong tendency to break down, despite their obvious appeal to the monopolistic mentality. The gentlemen in gentlemen's agreements, in other words, aren't always gentlemen. Said Smith:[2]

> In a free trade an effectual combination cannot
> be established but by the unanimous consent of
> every single trader, and it cannot last longer
> than every single trader continues of the same
> mind.

Thus the genius of U.S. antitrust policy is its pro-competition outlawing of price fixing and other cartel agreements and the rendering of such agreements as nonenforceable in courts of law. This is benign and most desirable regulation. Where applied antitrust departs

---

[1]*Wealth of Nations,* Modern Library, p. 128.
[2]*Ibid,* p. 129.

from genius is in its attempt to outlaw "incipient" monopoly.

Take, for instance, the district court's decision upsetting the proposed merger between Bethlehem Steel and Youngstown Sheet & Tube, a decision based in large part on the Celler-Kefauver antimerger amendment of 1950. The companies argued for "ultimate reckoning" —for consideration of the net effect on competition. In other words, since the proposed steel company would be a more efficient competitor to U.S. Steel and others, the merger would improve competition on balance. Yet the court rejected the merger on grounds that regardless of the net qualitative effects, any probable lessening of competition in a quantitative sense amounts to "incipient" monopoly, and is therefore illegal.

The antimerger Bethlehem-Youngstown decision represents an attack not only on an alleged "monopoly" position of the would-be merged firms but also, however inadvertently, on the ultimate steel consumer. For, in the final analysis, it is the American consumer himself—the car buyer, the apartment dweller, the appliance user, etc.—who must carry, through higher prices, the diseconomies of lower scale production resulting from the maintenance of separate enterprises that might more advantageously be merged.

But advantageous or not, only an unhampered market could decide the wisdom of a merger. For a big—perhaps the biggest—problem of applied antitrust is that of government omnipotence—the assumption that Congress, the regulatory agencies, and the courts can in fact spot actual "incipiency" and thereby hopefully improve on the market mechanism. The Antitrust Division is hardly so competent, for example, in steel technology and marketing as to be able to say just what organizational structure is economical in the production and marketing of steel, and what is not, notwithstanding a battery of government economists. The market test, on the other hand, would determine the rightness or wrongness of the merger of the two steel companies (which combined, incidentally, would still not have equaled U.S. Steel in size at the time of the merger proposal). Yet, as Judge Edward Weinfeld made clear in his decision barring the merger, he could not quite believe the market was able to make such a determination, especially not in the case of big business:[1]

> Congress in its efforts to preserve the free-enterprise system and the benefits to flow to the nation and to the consuming public did not, in enacting the antitrust laws, intend to give free play to the balancing power of gigantic enterprises and leave the less powerful purchaser helpless. What the Congress sought to preserve was a social and economic order not dependent on the power of the few to take care of themselves.

So bigness and fewness are subjected to close and suspicious scrutiny, especially when firms expand by acquisition or merger. Vertical, horizontal, and con-

---

[1] *U.S.* v. *Bethlehem Steel Corp.,* 168 F. Supp. 576, S.D.N.Y. (1958).

glomerate mergers—clearly signs of external corporate expansionism but not at all clearly signs of corporate monopoly—are nonetheless under an antitrust pale. (When a firm expands into another phase of an industry, say, from smelting copper into mining copper, this is vertical integration; when a firm expands along the same line of business, say, an A & P buying up (if antitrust would let it) a chain of supermarkets, it is a horizontal merger; and when a firm expands into an entirely different line of business, as in the case of General Tire buying out RKO, this is conglomerate integration.) But whatever the type of external integration, it is vulnerable to antitrust prosecution.

So, we see the Du Pont Company,[1] after thirteen years of litigation, forced to divest its "vertical" stock acquisition in General Motors, an acquisition made some forty years earlier. In its 1957 decision, the Supreme Court conceded that the executives of both firms had behaved "honorably and fairly," that General Motors—as an intermediate consumer, if a very large consumer—had not passed over considerations of "price, service and quality" in its purchases of Du Pont products; but nonetheless the High Court declared Du Pont's stock investment subject to "potential" abuse, and hence ruled it illegal, putting a lot of weight on a letter written by the late J. J. Raskob of Du Pont decades earlier. The letter, the Justice Department argued, was evidence of Du Pont's intent to exploit its GM stock ownership and foreclose markets by giving some special deals on Du

---

[1]*U.S.* v. *Du Pont,* 353 U.S. 586 (1957).

Pont products to GM purchasing agents.

In his dissent, Justice Harold Burton said that General Motors simply had not purchased exclusively or obtained privileged terms from Du Pont. Significantly, too, Justice Burton noted that the Clayton Act, especially Section 7, the authority under which the Supreme Court ordered Du Pont to liquidate its General Motors investment, was a "sleeping giant," and that all other corporate tie-ups, whether recent or ancient, whether by merger or by asset acquisition, whether vertical or horizontal or conglomerate integration, were now vulnerable to the giant's "newly discovered teeth." Now, practically any big business, perhaps out of favor with the administration in power or with the FTC or Antitrust Division, could be hailed into court, charged with fostering "incipient" monopoly and conceivably broken up. In fact, according to a *Wall Street Journal* story in 1967, the Antitrust Division was found to be keeping a fat "war file" on General Motors and its half-share of the American auto market for the time when and if the division goes to court to break up the auto giant. But such antitrust concepts of "size," "shares," and "concentration" add up to fuzzy economics on the nature of competition and cast doubt on the economic soundness of Section 7 of the Clayton Act, as amended.

There is another rub with Section 7 of the Clayton Act: the weakening of the Anglo-American legal tradition that under the rule of *corpus delicti* proof of wrongdoing must be clear and actual, not probable or hypothetical. But in the world of antitrust, a merger is potentially illegal when its effect "may" be substantially to lessen competition or "tend" to create a monopoly.

Senator Joseph O'Mahoney of Wyoming, a staunch friend of a strong antitrust policy, saw a trap in the word "may." During the debate on the Celler-Kefauver amendment in 1949 he said:[1]

> The difference between the word "will" and the word "may" is almost as great as the distinction between the poles.... I prefer the word "will" to the word "may"; because if we use the word "may," no one under the sun can tell what the law means, because "may" conveys into the hands of some future Federal Trade Commission the power to hold...practices to be illegal, although the Federal Trade Commission now says they are not illegal.

The ambiguity in amended Section 7 goes beyond the words "may" and "tend." The language provides no fixed criteria for what is understood by the phrases "line of commerce," "section of the country," or "substantially to lessen competition." Are polyethylene film and cellophane, for example, in the same "line of commerce"? Is a "section of the country" a town, city, county, state, or multistate area? And just how substantial is "substantially"? Hardly any lawyers or economists would view these terms in the same way. The upshot is more entanglement in the arbitrary mire of administrative law. Said one of the authors of the Celler-Kefauver amendment, Congressman Emanuel Celler, during the House debate:[2]

---

[1]*Congressional Record,* August 12, 1949, p. 11344.
[2]*Congressional Record,* July 7, 1949, p. 9061.

The phrase "to restrain commerce in any section of the country" is new phraseology. I have not heard that before in any antitrust legislation or in any Federal Trade Commission legislation. It would give rise to all manner of questions, of controversies, and of disputes; there would be nothing but confusion. It would mean a field day for the lawyers.

Moreover, although bigness is said not to be a crime, it would appear that it really is from assorted antitrust attacks on such giants as Standard Oil (N.J.), General Motors, IBM, United States Steel, General Electric, Procter and Gamble, Eastman Kodak, Manufacturers-Hanover Trust, Alcoa, Union Carbide, A & P, and so on. In the case of GM, for instance, a grand jury indicted the firm on charges of monopolizing the production and sale of Diesel locomotives. The indictment charged GM with capture of 80 percent of the Diesel locomotive market "through the use of its vast economic power," to quote from the *Annual Report* of the Attorney General for 1961. Yet who captured whom? Railroads, not exactly *small* businesses, bought from GM so as to get the most for the least, to economize on the cost of locomotives.

And we see IBM[1] under an antitrust pale, in 1952 (and again in 1969), not for any overt act of monopoly or any "intent" to monopolize, but for the "fact" of "monopoly"—the fact being that IBM had simply be-

---

[1]*U.S.* v. *International Business Machines Corp.*, Civil Action No. 72-344, January 21, 1952.

come too big, had won a heavy majority share of the punched-card business. IBM at the time commented:[1]

> The Government saw the advantages of using our machines plus the service which we always give; and they increased their business with us until, as they state, 95 percent of their punched-card machines are IBMs. Consequently, if the Government accuses us of being a monopoly, they are themselves co-defendant. Can anyone conceive of the Government's being forced to use our machines to this extent?

In the Paramount Pictures case, a vertical integration case, five major motion picture producer-distributor-exhibitor companies—Paramount, RKO, Loew's, Warner Bros., and Twentieth-Century-Fox—were found guilty of vertical integration by engaging in the movie business from the story conference in Hollywood to selling tickets at the box office on Main Street. Consider the language of the Supreme Court's decision:[2]

> First, [vertical integration] runs afoul of the Sherman Act if it was a calculated scheme to gain control over an appreciable segment of the market and to restrain or suppress competition, rather than an expansion to meet legitimate business needs. . . . Second, a vertically integrated enterprise, like other aggregations of

---

[1]Quoted by Thomas and Marva Belden, *The Lengthening Shadow*, Little, Brown, 1962, p. 297.
[2]*U.S.* v. *Paramount Pictures,* 334 U.S. 131 (1948).

business units *(United States* v. *Aluminum Co.
of America)* will constitute monopoly which,
though unexercised, violates the Sherman Act
provided a power to exclude competition is
coupled with a purpose or intent to do so. As
we pointed out in *United States* v. *Griffith, . . .*
size is itself an earmark of monopoly power.
For size carries with it an opportunity for abuse.
And the fact that the power created by size was
utilized in the past to crush or prevent competition is potent evidence that the requisite purpose or intent attends the presence of monopoly
power.

Now it should be self-evident that all competitors
long "to gain control over an appreciable segment of
the market," and whether a "calculated scheme" or not,
is this wrong? If it is, then all competition—which tran-
scends, by the way, economics and is to be found in
sports, love, education, art, politics, in practically every
human endeavor and in virtually all of nature—is somehow also wrong. The incongruity of the Sherman Act,
as currently interpreted, lies in what amounts to its
stern command to businessmen: Compete but do not
win; don't make the product so good or sell it so cheap
that you obtain a dominant share of the market. But as
for bigness being "an earmark of monopoly power,"
size is a function of the job to be done, of the economies
of scale—of which the market, really the consumer, is
the final arbiter.

Integration, when feasible, as it oftentimes is, usually

involves cost savings—the elimination of waste. Yet whatever the integration—vertical, horizontal, or conglomerate—the main check on its economic virtue or lack of it is not, or perhaps more accurately, ought not to be, antitrust. The check should be the consumer. If he approves an integration, he will say so—through his purchases; if he disapproves, he will also say so—through his nonpurchases.

Thus, perhaps the error of applied—really misapplied—antitrust lies in its fundamental misunderstanding of the market. Judge Learned Hand exemplified this basic misunderstanding in the *Alcoa* case, arguing in effect that Alcoa's competitiveness and superior service to the consumer in steadily reducing the cost of aluminum from dollars per pound to cents per pound was somehow bad:[1]

> [Alcoa] insists that it never excluded competitors; but we can think of no more effective exclusion than progressively to embrace each new opportunity as it opened, and to face every newcomer with new capacity already geared into a great organization having the advantage of experience, trade connections, and the elite of personnel.

Pricing, whether "predatory," "uniform," "discriminatory," or "administered," is another concern of the antitrusters. Predatory pricing figured in the *Standard Oil* case of 1911, one of the grandfather cases. In this

---

[1]*U.S.* v. *Aluminum Co. of America*, 148 F. (2d) 416, 427 (1945).

antitrust suit the government alleged that the Standard
Oil Company engaged in "predatory" pricing activities
—that is, the firm deliberately underpriced in specific
locations in order to destroy smaller competitors, and
overpriced in other less competitive locations. Then,
after the targeted competitors were out of the way, the
company would presumably recoup any losses by raising
prices to "monopoly" levels. After a painstaking analysis of the case, however, economist John S. McGee concluded: [1]

> Judging from the record, Standard Oil did not
> use predatory price discrimination to drive out
> competing refiners, nor did its pricing practice
> have that effect. Whereas there may be a very
> few cases in which retail kerosene peddlers or
> dealers went out of business after or during
> price cutting, there is no real proof that Stand-
> ard's pricing policies were responsible. I am
> convinced that Standard did not systematically,
> if ever, use local price cutting in retailing, or
> anywhere else, to reduce competition. To do so
> would have been foolish; and whatever else has
> been said about them, the old Standard organ-
> ization was seldom criticized for making less
> money when it could readily have made more.

Consider: In order for a firm to practice predatory
pricing, the barriers against market entry must be abso-

---

[1]"Predatory Price Cutting," *The Journal of Law and Economics,*
October 1958, p. 168.

lute. If this is not the case, the ability to control supply would be incomplete and the monopoly would cease to exist. Further, there is sometimes little to prevent a competitor from temporarily withdrawing from a "price war," only to return when prices are restabilized at a profitable level. Again, the predatory price cutter can himself be hit with retaliation by similar localized price cutting in his own backyard by another large firm. Moreover, the regular customers of the predatory price cutter are not likely to take kindly to news of discriminatory price cuts elsewhere. About the only happy party in "price wars" is the consumer, a price-war profiteer; to him the lower the price the better.

In the long run, realization of profits by Standard Oil, over and above the profits realized in industries of comparable risk, had precisely the same effect in the oil industry as in other industries. These profits acted as a lure to investment, with the result that investment syndicates with huge financial reserves backed new firms in the oil industry like Gulf and Texaco—not exactly small businesses either—so that the giant Standard Oil Company could not long, even if it wanted to, predatorily cut prices, not with a giant Gulf or Texaco or even small independents to take it on.

For competition is not a matter of numbers or of smallness, bigness, magnitude of capital requirements, or, as the term is frequently defined, fairness. Instead, competition consists of voluntary economic dealings of people with each other, the absence of fraud, theft, coercion, misrepresentation, or intimidation, which if present are matters for the courts. It is, in other words,

essentially freedom to sell and freedom to buy, freedom
of entry for firms into industries and buyers into markets.
Negation of competition, on the other hand, is denial of
freedom of entry—a denial that only government can
maintain in a free society. To endure, in other words,
monopoly needs the protection of government by such
means as licenses, regulations, and protective tariffs. As
the great seventeenth century jurist, Lord Coke, noted[1]

> A monopoly is an institution or allowance by
> the king, by his grant, commission, or otherwise
> . . . to any person or persons, bodies politic or
> corporate, for the sole buying, selling, making,
> working, or using of anything, whereby any
> other person or persons, body politic or corpo-
> rate, are sought to be restrained of any freedom
> or liberty that they had before, or hindered in
> their lawful trade.

Again, steep capital requirements seem irrelevant to
the vigor of competition. Many hold that the hundreds
of millions of dollars required to put up, say, a steel
mill, an aluminum smelter, or an automobile assembly
plant automatically makes for oligopoly—oligopoly, of
course, representing the antitrust crime of fewness of
sellers. But these few are generally the victors in the
competitive struggle. And, when the occasion requires,
as in the cases of computers, xerography and 60-second
cameras, Wall Street seems quite ready, willing and

---

[1]Quoted in Richard T. Ely and others, *Outlines of Economics,*
3rd ed., Macmillan, 1917, pp. 190-91.

able to finance yet another enterprising idea, no matter how big. Smaller companies can also join forces for financial strength and resort to the joint-venture route as have Olin Mathieson Chemical and Revere Copper & Brass to form Ormet Corporation, a big integrated aluminum joint-venture company, and as have American Viscose and Sun Oil to form Avi-Sun, a joint-venture plastics company.

Further, an "industry," let alone a "market," does not at all lend itself to easy and precise definition. Market fences separating industries are continually falling away. Plastics companies have captured many steel markets; chemical companies have scored with plastics; rubber, distilling, steel, and meat-packing companies have gone into chemicals; oil companies are invading rubber markets; aircraft concerns manufacture hydrofoil boats; telephone companies are moving into data-processing transmission, and so on. As a result, a given industry becomes an elusive entity, statistically, legally, and conceptually, especially over time. In 1956, for instance, the Supreme Court held that Du Pont's three-quarter share of the U.S. cellophane market did not constitute a monopoly. The Court held Du Pont's cellophane, in accounting for only one-sixth of the total market for some dozen different flexible wrappings, certainly did not constitute a monopolistic market share.[1] Du Pont itself exemplifies the difficulty of industrial classification. Most industry classifiers place it in the "chemical" industry, but it also properly belongs to

---

[1] *U.S.* v. *E. I. Du Pont,* 351 U.S. 377 (1956).

a host of other "industries"—textiles, explosives, paint, drugs, plastics, metals, photographic film, and so on.

To be sure, antitrusters and others may deduce from corporate size—"corporate giantism"—and fewness of industry numbers—"concentration"—that each firm has some specific market share, that producers collectively are in control of the market, and that perhaps market shares are the result of some kind of producer allocation. If all this were true, surely the giants would have been able to control their fate over the years.

Yet a look at a 1954 Brookings Institution study,[1] updated in 1964, would reveal that the top is a slippery place. The study by economist A.D.H. Kaplan, recalling such now-forgotten industry giants as American Locomotive, American Woolen, and American Molasses, showed that big businesses are anything but insulated from competition and fast-moving technology, that the industry colossus of one decade can become the sick firm of the next, that the "basic" industry of one era can be replaced by another "basic" industry in a new era.

Current antitrust, however, frequently tries to arrest change, to freeze the status quo, to extrapolate a static view of existing market conditions into a supposedly changeless future. But the present as well as the future is always changing in our dynamic economic world to meet ever-new conditions.

Accordingly the Supreme Court's "rule of reason" of 1911 should be reaffirmed. Section 7 of the Clayton Act and its 1950 amendment—the Celler-Kefauver Anti-

---

[1]A. D. H. Kaplan, *Big Enterprise in a Competitive System,* The Brookings Institution, 1954 and 1964.

merger Act—unreasonably restrain trade and should therefore be repealed, with Sections 1 and 2 of the Sherman Act serving in their stead. Interventionistic antitrust can become benign antitrust when it catches up with the world as it is.

CHAPTER IV

Consumer Protectionism and the Federal Trade Commission

An enterprise system is a system of voluntary contract. Neither fraud nor coercion is within the ethics of the market system. Indeed there is no possibility of coercion in a pure enterprise system because the competition of rivals provides alternatives to every buyer or seller. All real economic systems contain some monopoly, and hence some coercive power for particular individuals, but the amount and extent of such monopoly power are usually much exaggerated, and in any case monopoly is not an integral part of the logic of the system.

—George J. Stigler,
*The Intellectual and
the Market Place*

While, according to one American President, the business of America is business, part of the game, political and otherwise, apparently is alternately to knock and faintly praise business and then tie it up in regulatory knots. And this is about par for the Washington way. Take the 1912 presidential campaign as a case in point. One of the key issues of the campaign was trust-busting —an issue with reverberations, if with different semantics, continuing down to the present.

In the 1912 campaign, Democratic candidate Woodrow Wilson charged Bull Mooser and trust-buster extraordinary Theodore Roosevelt with "coming to terms" with the monopolists. For his part, Roosevelt said in pre-Galbraithian tones that monopoly was inevitable, that industrial monopoly should be publicly acknowledged and publicly regulated. So from every side, though least from William Howard Taft and the regular Republicans, industry was the whipping boy. Wilson charged that industry had indeed become dominant, that the American citizen had lost his traditional economic freedom, that in an age of giantism the individual no longer could enter any business he pleased and succeed or fail on his own merits.

Candidate Wilson also said—me-tooed by candidate Roosevelt—that the Sherman Act of 1890 and the Supreme Court's Standard Oil "rule of reason" decision of 1911 were no longer adequate to stop or impede the supposed cancer-like growth of monopoly, that new laws were necessary to cope with the quickly deteriorating competitive situation, that, among other things, a watchdog commission was necessary to police competition in order to save it.

Thus, two new supposedly competition-saving laws were passed shortly after the accession of President Wilson to office—the previously mentioned Federal Trade Commission and Clayton Acts of 1914. The FTC Act created a watchdog commission to attempt to elevate the plane of competition, investigate and prevent "unfair" methods of competition, and eliminate practices which "lessened" competition. The Wheeler-Lea Act of 1938 further empowered the FTC to require discontinuance of commercial practices held injurious or unfair to consumers even when competition is unaffected, and enabled the FTC to seek to prevent false or deceptive advertising of drugs, foods, cosmetics, and corrective or curative devices.

In addition, the Federal Trade Commission Act of 1914 gives the FTC coordinate power with the Justice Department to enforce the Clayton Antitrust Act. Enforcement powers consist of informal and formal means. Informally the FTC moves upon getting complaints from consumers, from one competitor against another, and from other complainers, including newspapers and magazines. The FTC looks into the complaint, frequently discusses the problem with the accused business firm and may then issue a "letter of discontinuance." If the firm countersigns the letter, thereby agreeing to discontinue the offending practice, the entire matter is dropped.

Formally, the FTC may issue a complaint against an alleged violator and assign the case to an FTC hearing examiner. The examiner conducts a hearing and renders an initial decision which may involve an order to the errant firm to cease and desist from a particular business action or practice. This decision becomes binding, in the name of the commission, thirty days after it is filed; but any party to the proceeding may appeal the decision to the commission, and beyond that, under certain conditions, to the courts.

Today the FTC is housed in its own headquarters building at Pennsylvania Avenue and Sixth Street in Washington, D.C. The building is a "symbol," said President Franklin D. Roosevelt righteously in the building dedication ceremonies on July 12, 1937, "of the purpose of Government to insist on a greater application of the Golden Rule to the conduct of corporations and business enterprises in their relationship to the body politic." The commission is run by a bipartisan agency of five members, of which not more than three may be of the same political party, appointed by the President for seven-year terms with the advice and consent of the Senate.

Some idea of the work of the commission can be seen in the partial listing of its various divisions, as follows:

Division of Consent Orders
Division of Trade Regulation Rules
Division of Advisory Opinions and Guides
Division of Trade Practice Conferences
Division of Mergers
Division of General Trade Restraints
Division of Discriminatory Practices
Division of Accounting
Division of Compliance
Division of Scientific Operations
Division of Textiles and Furs Enforcement
Division of Textiles and Furs Regulation

Division of Economic Evidence
Division of Financial Statistics
Division of Economic Reports

What is the *raison d'être* of these divisions? Broadly they have two duties: One is trade regulation—dealing with so-called unfair business methods; the other is anti-trust—dealing with Clayton Act and Robinson-Patman violations, as discussed, in part, in the previous chapter on antitrust.

In the area of trade regulation, for example, the FTC monitors radio and television commercials and advertisements in newspapers, magazines, handbills, and other printed material. The FTC "requests" all radio and TV networks to submit all commercial scripts broadcast in a single week of each month, and newspapers and magazines to submit a similar sampling of their printed advertisements. Submissions based on these requests enabled the FTC to cast its Cyclopian eye in one recent twelve-month period on, according to its own count, 516,352 radio and TV commercial scripts and 302,572 printed advertisements. From these totals, 61,300 advertisements were further examined for possible corrective action by the legal staff.

One upshot of the FTC advertising surveillance is the celebrated case of the Colgate Rapid Shave TV commercial. The commercial showed "sandpaper" being shaved clean of sand with ease and dispatch after an application of the shaving cream. But the FTC investigated and found, alas, that not sandpaper was used in the demonstration but a sheet of plexiglass coated with sand. The commission decided that the commercial was "deceptive and misleading."[1] the company and its advertising agency—respectively Colgate-Palmolive and Ted Bates & Co.—pleaded that sandpaper did not photograph well, that some dramatic latitude in this instance had to be allowed for the television medium. The plea did not work; a cease and desist order was issued; and the company and agency took the case to court, with ultimately the Supreme Court itself upholding the commission and the Yale, Columbia, Notre Dame, and University of California-Los Angeles law reviews publishing learned articles on Colgate's lathery puff.

Yet while wise judges and legal scholars mull the niceties of law and the mores of advertising, some rather hard questions persist: Has the FTC crossed over into the field of censorship? How far must realism in sales promotion be taken to please the FTC? And, indeed, can the seller, from lover to politician, be denied some puffery in his promotion? To do so would be a denial of human nature, a denial that Walter Mitty with his daydreams is Mr. Everyman, a denial that the politician has been above blarney, perenially selling peace and prosperity and two chickens in every pot, a denial that the lover also has engaged in his share of hokum, telling his beloved that she is the most dazzling female since Cleopatra. So, too, has the businessman been puffing his wares as the "finest," the "best," the "greatest," the "biggest," and so on. At the same time, the businessman of course should not puff his way into definitive mis-

---

[1] FTC Dockets 5972 and 5986.

representation—the used car dealer, for example, saying that an automobile has been driven only five thousand miles (the odometer so changed to read) when in fact it has been driven, say, twenty thousand miles. If any businessman does in fact misrepresent—and, sadly, a number do—the courts should throw the book at him.

Getting back to the Rapid Shave commercial, must all mockups in television or magazine advertising be condemned as unreal? The marbles in the Campbell Soup ad, for example? Must real flowers—which would wilt under hot studio lights—be used in a perfume commercial? Can an offstage fan substitute for the wind in a model's hair? Can the model in the tea commercial smile with satisfaction while sipping tinted water held to be more photogenic than iced tea? Would the charge of deception be raised when a child is shown enjoying oatmeal or spinach?

The antideception powers conferred on the FTC by the Wool Products Labeling Act of 1939, the Fur Products Labeling Act of 1951, and the Textile Fiber Products Identification Act of 1958 also pose some rather odd problems. Merchants may think that it is hardly deceptive to label something as fake when it is not the real thing. But not the FTC. The commission has frowned on advertising and labeling of coats made with synthetic fur as "fake fur," "bogus fur," or "simulated fur." Yet under FTC rules advertisers are not prohibited from referring to "artificial flowers," "simulated pearls," "fake lizard," or "mock alligator."

It is apparently safe to say "fabric that looks like fur," or even to use "fur-like." The Red Fox Overall run-in with the FTC is instructive. The Georgia manufacturer who had been producing Red Fox overalls for some three decades was charged by the FTC with practicing deception because his overalls were cotton garments containing no fox fur whatever. Ordered by the commission to change the brand name, the manufacturer appealed to his two U.S. senators who promptly introduced bills in the Senate to prevent such treatment, whereupon the FTC suddenly saw the error of its ways, understandably reversed itself, and quashed the order.[1] Yet how far should a literal interpretation of brand names be carried? Might the consumer be deceived, for example, in learning that Star-Kist tuna has not in fact been kissed by a star, or that Log Cabin maple syrup is not produced in a log cabin, or that Old Gold cigarettes contain no gold at all?

Meanwhile, the synthetic fur industry has been more than slightly confused by one FTC ruling which states that the industry's advertising must not carry any "names, words, deceptions, descriptive matter, or other symbols which connote or signify a fur-bearing animal." This rule has complicated the marketing of acrylic fabrics which closely resemble real fur and are a boon to the consumer who would like the look of fur but rather not pay the price of real fur. Also understandably interested in the rule are acrylic producers such as American Cyanamid (Creslan), Dow Chemical (Zefran), Tennessee Eastman (Verel), Union Carbide (Dynel), Du Pont (Orlon), and Chemstrand (Acrilan).

Maybe humor is the answer. Union Carbide's adver-

---

[1]*Barron's,* February 24, 1964.

tising agency, Chirurg & Cairns, Inc. of New York, joshed the FTC with the publication of its "A First Primer on Fur Fakery with Lessons on Beating about the Bush." Some of its suggestions for avoiding possible FTC charges were such phrases as "Big Game Fashions," "Jungle Jackets," "Impish Imposters," "Bogus Beauties," "Flattering Forgeries," and "Zoo Spots." The agency also ran full-page color ads in the *New Yorker* and *Vogue* with photographs of a model wearing what looked like a fur coat. The headline caption read: "It isn't fake anything. It's real Dynel."

Because of its pervasiveness, advertising receives the brunt of the FTC's antideception crusade. By the FTC's own estimate, about one-third of its annual appropriation is spent to inhibit the "cheating" of consumers, principally by false or deceptive advertising. Among the targets are ads relating to food supplements such as vitamins and vitamin-mineral combinations, food plans and freezers, air purifiers, pesticide preparations, products said to promise a "cure" or at least "quick relief" from baldness and the common cold, mail-order real estate sales of land in the snow-free areas of the South and Southwest, along with ads said to exaggerate the performance of toys, aluminum siding, clear plastic "storm windows," "debt consolidation" services, "surplus" radios, and other items, probably including good old-fashioned snake oil. Among what the FTC labels as "sucker sales" are: "Buy now or lose the chance . . . ," "You have been specially selected . . . ," "Just a few easy lessons . . . ," "You can save up to . . . ," "Yours absolutely free. . . ."

The FTC drive for truth-in-advertising helped trig-

ger the truth-in-packaging crusade in Congress. Mis-
labeled, slack-filled packages are of course censurable;
and ingredients-contents labeling is welcome and benign
regulation. But still one wonders how sure-fire are FDA-
and FTC-like solutions to the problem, including consumer package labeling of chemical compounds. As one
lady cosmetic executive told a Senate Commerce subcommittee on legislation to standardize and secure
"fair" packaging and labeling of consumer products:
"The cosmetic industry could hardly advertise 'She's
lovely, she's engaged, she uses polyakylene glycol, pro-
pylene glycol, and propyl parahydroxy benzoate'." The
executive explained that women really don't care about
the chemical composition of cosmetics. What women
purchase, she explained, is "a look, a feeling, a promise,
an idea, a state of mind. Frankly, I call it . . . hope."[1]

Or, to take another example of the strained meaning
of truth-in-advertising, the FTC and the Book-of-the-
Month Club fought over the word "free" all the way up
to the Supreme Court. The club offered membership—
or sold books—on the basis of a minimum annual purchase of a certain number of books for which the member got an additional book or books "free." Now, to be
sure, ran the club's defense, this "free" does not mean
literally free—i.e., free of cost; for there was a specific
quid pro quo carefully spelled out in the application
form, the formal purchase agreement. And, after all,
just how free is free? The economist sagely says there is
no such thing as a free lunch. Yet government literature

---

[1]*New York Times,* May 23, 1965.

refers continually—without fear of FTC censure of course—to our "free" schools, "free" roads, "free" parks, "free" libraries, and so on. Still, so far the FTC has issued no order forbidding such government puffery, while an order banishing the word "free" from Book-of-the-Month Club advertising was issued. But FTC Commissioner Lowell B. Mason saw red and dissented from the cease and desist order, commenting:[1]

> By this order the Commission sets itself up as a lexicographer with power to punish those who ignore our definitions. By this order the Commission has fallen into the one-word, one-meaning fallacy which all semanticists regard as futile. Serious students of the problem hold that words shift and change in meaning. . . . It is not the function of the Commission to define and limit the use of subjective words. . . . We supplant accepted usage with bureaucratic fiat. And that I am against.

Advertised or displayed pricing may also be bureaucratically branded as deceptive and incur the wrath of the FTC. In such cases as *Regina Corp.* (FTC Docket 8323) and *Helbros Watch* (FTC Docket 6807), e.g., the FTC strongly objected to what it calls "fictitious" pricing, usually through the practices of manufacturers preticketing prices or of retailers advertising or displaying "manufacturer's list price" or "manufacturer's suggested price." Such prices are looked upon by the

---

[1]Lowell B. Mason, *The Language of Dissent,* World, 1959, p. 179.

FTC as unreal when they are deemed not to be the going trade or retail prices. In 1971 the FTC proposed a ban on automobile manufacturers' suggested retail or "sticker" prices which were deemed higher than prices actually charged in a substantial number of sales.

The FTC also turns a suspicious eye on cash savings claims on packages or display ads, especially those in which the retailer compares a higher price ("was," "usually," "regularly," "manufacturer's list price," and kindred designations) to his lower offering price (perhaps described as "now only," "sale price," "reduced to," "special," etc).[1] And the commission turns a suspicious eye on advertised pricing which includes such words as "free," "two-for-one," "half-price sale," "1¢ sale," "$1 sale," "50¢ off," "10¢ off," and similar language.

In addition, unproved advertising claims are condemned. In *Smith-Corona* (FTC Stipulation 9429), for example, the commission, without tongue in cheek, had the typewriter company agree no longer to represent its portable as resulting in higher grades or academic improvement without regard to the aptitude of the student or to the subject taught. In this vein the commission called upon the advertiser of *Rybutol* to stop claiming that the product will help prevent tiredness or loss of happiness, unless the advertising also disclosed that in most cases such symptoms are due to causes other than vitamin deficiency, and in such cases the product would be of little benefit. The *Rybutol* case

---

[1]FTC *Annual Report,* 1962, p. 5.

is not too far a cry from the commissioner's first three formal complaints issued on February 16, 1916, against three sellers for representing their cotton products as "cilk." The three respondents were ordered to "forthwith cease and desist . . . using the word 'cilk' in reference to any of their products other than silk. . . ."

More recently the FTC followed up the U.S. Surgeon General's Committee on Smoking and Health report on tobacco and cancer with a requirement that every cigarette package carry a warning that "cigarette smoking is hazardous to health," but Congress diluted the "is" to "may be." The commission has also considered rules that would prohibit any suggestion in advertisements that cigarettes produce a sense of physical well-being or that any one cigarette is less harmful than another. The Tobacco Institute, whose members include the major cigarette manufacturers, objected to the proposed rules, arguing that such restrictions might reduce cigarette advertising to a bleak statement of the brand name plus the commission-required warning that smoking is a health hazard. The Federal Communications Commission has gone even further by banning radio and TV cigarette commercials altogether.

In any event, the commission's approach to deception and false advertising is, it seems, one of right ends and wrong means. Outright deception and misrepresentation should of course be illegal, and here the FTC is on solid ground. But for all the wrangling between the commission and industry, for all of the FTC's investigations and cease and desist orders, for all its stipulations and complaints, the old Latin precept of *caveat emptor* seems to be the key workable rule of the marketplace. People are not domesticated animals or hothouse plants to be shielded from every risk of the marketplace by an all-wise magnanimous and benevolent commission. It is unrealistic that cigarette smokers have not heard of the well-publicized connection between cancer and smoking. Advertising can hardly be tailored for semimorons, even though in some senses, it often seems to be.

Truth in advertising is a good thing and so is truth in politics, but to in effect reduce cigarette advertising to "Smoke X Cigarettes—Even If They Kill You" is extreme. Similar warnings can be attached to whiskey bottles or inserted in airline advertising. All of life is a calculated risk. The FTC could conceivably order each baby tattooed at birth with "Danger, Death Ahead," and the label could not be faulted for lack of truth. Smoking is a risk of life, and there are many such risks. To smoke or not to smoke would seem to be a problem for the individual.

Yet FTC Chairman Paul Rand Dixon had a point and delineated a legitimate stamping—if swampy—ground for commission concern when he said:[1]

> Let's face it, a great deal of advertising is aimed at the optimism of the credulous rather than at the minds of the skeptical. For this reason, the Federal Trade Commission cannot be as tolerant of "harmless" exaggerations of material fact as some advertisers and their agencies might

---

[1]FTC release, March 15, 1963.

wish. [The marketplace sees cases of] old people who invest their life savings in vending machines, the boys who waste time, money, and hope on phoney correspondence schools, the housewives who are baited into buying sewing machines and freezers they can't afford, and countless other gyps.

Still, for all the good counsel and policy in the Dixon statement, government, like every other social institution, is human and also errant, with errant governmental puffery quite material and not by any means necessarily harmless. Is Old Age and Survivors Insurance, for example, really insurance? Are we un-American by the lights of the Buy American Act when we buy Irish linen, Brazilian coffee, or Danish silver? Is the Fair Labor Standards Act really fair? Did the Lend-Lease Act of World War II really lend and lease?

If Chairman Dixon places such stress on the "optimism of the credulous" and their frequent inability to distinguish between a puff and a genuine claim, can he really tolerate the more complex demands of political democracy in which the citizen is expected to cut through the puffery of government and party politics and decide matters of far greater moment than whether a detergent washes whiter than white or a mouthwash will convert the bridesmaid into a bride? Certainly the "rule of reason" should apply to both political and commercial advertising.

Now, what about the FTC's second major role—antitrust—about which we've already commented some in the previous chapter? Consider, for example, its policy on the businessman's use of tying contracts, presumably a practice that could lead to diminution of competition. In 1920, for example, the Supreme Court upheld a lower court's reversal of an FTC order against Gratz. This manufacturer of both bands and wrapping material used in baling cotton, would not sell one product without the other, thereby "tying" the two goods together in a supposed violation of the Federal Trade Commission Act Section 5 on unfair methods of competition. Thus, in *FTC* v. *Gratz*,[1] an ancient case but one which still very much illustrates current FTC thinking on competition and monopoly, the Supreme Court saw little that was unfair in the practice and affirmed the lower court's reversal. The majority, speaking through Justice McReynolds, held that Gratz had a monopoly of neither the "tied" nor the "tying" good.

But Justice Brandeis most presciently dissented, maintaining that Section 5 was designed to nip monopoly in the bud and not allow it to become full-blown, that the FTC proceedings are not "punitive" but "preventive" of monopoly. The Brandeis opinion would seem to assume clairvoyance on the part of the FTC to sift potential monopolistic trade practices from innocent and even really competitive practices. To argue Gratz was a potential monopolist is prejudging the future, displaying an omnicompetence not given even to appointed guardians of competition.

The Supreme Court followed up its logic of *FTC* v.

---

[1] 253 U.S. 421 (1920).

Gratz in *FTC* v. *Sinclair Refining,* again upsetting an FTC order on a supposedly unfair method of competition and sustaining the contractual right of Sinclair to insist to its franchised dealers that only Sinclair gas be sold through Sinclair pumps,[1] a most reasonable insistence one would think, the FTC of the 1920s notwithstanding. But the FTC of the 1960s resurrected after four decades the idea that a franchisor does not have the right of product control over his franchise dealers. Specifically, the FTC questioned the right of the Carvel Corp., an East Coast, soft ice cream dispensing franchisor, to require that only Carvel's ice cream and not somebody else's be sold by Carvel dealers through Carvel dispensers in Carvel cups. Carvel won its case in court,[2] and for this the FTC should have been pleased that the consumer was not misled into believing he was consuming Carvel ice cream when in fact he might have been consuming a mislabelled product. Here is a case in which apparently one arm of the FTC—trade regulation—was not aware of what the other arm—antitrust—was doing.

Price "discrimination," unless warranted by provable cost savings, is another trade practice looked upon as dubious by the FTC. The commission takes its policy directive from Section 2 of the Clayton Act as amended by the Robinson-Patman Act of 1936. But calculation of costs, and especially cost allocation, is anything but a precise science, and the FTC has haggled long and hard

---

[1]261 U.S. 463 (1923).
[2]206 F. Supp. 636 (S.D.N.Y. 1963).

with industry as to what are true costs. Old Section 2
of the Clayton Act was fuzzy enough and said in part:

> It shall be unlawful . . . to discriminate in price
> between different purchasers. . . where the ef-
> fect . . . may be substantially to lessen competi-
> tion or tend to create a monopoly in any line of
> commerce. . . [provided] that nothing herein
> contained shall prevent discrimination in price
> . . . on account of differences in the grade, qual-
> ity, or quantity of the commodity sold.

New Section 2 of the Clayton Act, as amended by
Robinson-Patman, put into the law a phrase that rendered price discrimination far more vulnerable to FTC
attack, for the quantity discount proviso was changed
to hold that volume discounts are not lawful if they can
be construed to be injurious to competition. The uneasy
out for the discounter is to justify his discounts on the
basis of actual cost savings.

Quantity discounts and private branding were both
at issue in the *Goodyear-Sears* case in 1933. The rubber
company sold tires with the Sears trademark to the
retailer on the basis of cost plus 6 percent. The FTC
issued a complaint charging price discrimination and
contending that the tires were very much like those
Goodyear marketed through its own twenty-five thousand dealers, differing only in trademark, tread patterns, and, above all, in price. The price discrimination
amounted to between 12 and 22 percent in favor of
Sears. Goodyear appealed to the courts, and the FTC

order was reversed by the circuit court of appeals.[1]

But if the FTC was unsuccessful in its initial attempt to stop what it regarded as the illicit relationship between Goodyear and Sears, the case appears to have been an important factor in the passage of the Robinson-Patman Act of 1936. Robinson-Patman, an act which carries vestiges of the old National Industrial Recovery Act in which selling-prices below *full* cost were regarded as antisocial, was designed, as noted, to reinforce the original Section 2 of the Clayton Act on price discrimination, and the amended section gave the FTC strong authority to move against Goodyear and all other alleged price discriminators.

For another lesson on the FTC approach to price discrimination, look into the Morton Salt[2] case in which the FTC charged the company with discrimination in pricing among different buyers of its table salt of like grade and quality through the following volume discount schedule:

	Price per Case
Less-than-carload purchases	$1.60
Carload purchases	1.50
5,000-case purchases in any consecutive 12 months	1.40
50,000-case purchases in any consecutive 12 months	1.35

---

[1]*Goodyear Tire* v. *FTC,* 92 F. (2d) 677 (1937).
[2]*FTC* v. *Morton Salt,* 334 U.S. 37 (1948).

Aghast at the plight of small grocers, the FTC determined that only giant food chains, i.e., only five purchasers—American Stores, National Tea, Safeway, A & P, and Kroger—ever bought Morton Salt in a great enough volume to qualify for the lowest discount price, $1.35 per case. The commission then jumped to the conclusion that competition had somehow been "injured"—translation: small food distributors had been injured—and, accordingly, a cease and desist order was issued against the offending salt company. In hearings, as a justification for the discounts, the company attempted to prove genuine cost savings but the FTC overruled the defense. The company carried the case all the way to the Supreme Court, but the Court was unimpressed by the firm's contention that a chain buying fifty thousand cases of salt per year is creating substantial economies of scale for the seller and is clearly entitled to a discount beyond that available to the independent retailer and smaller jobber and wholesaler. The Court somehow contended that Robinson-Patman

> does not require that the discriminations must in fact have harmed competition, but only that there is a reasonable possibility that they "may" have such an effect . . . . The Commission is authorized by the Act to bar discriminatory prices upon the "reasonable possibility" that different prices for like goods to competing purchasers may have the defined effect on competition.

The Court's play on the word "possibility" as opposed to the word "probability" accounted, in part, for the dissent by Justice Jackson who held that Robinson-Patman called for a reasonable *probability* of injury to competition. Plainly, as the majority opinion of the Supreme Court in effect indicated, Robinson-Patman was designed in large measure to penalize the chains—and, however inadvertently, the consumer as well—and to rescue the independent grocers, druggists, and other small distributors from the rigors of competition.

A more recent Robinson-Patman rescue of a small company from the rigors of competition was upheld by the Supreme Court in its 1967 decision in the case of *Utah Pie Co.* v. *Continental Baking Co., et al.*[1] Utah Pie claimed it had been damaged by a pie price-cutting war fought in the frozen food cases of the supermarkets of Salt Lake City by Continental Baking, Carnation Co., and Pet, Inc. against each other and against little Utah Pie. Utah Pie, said the Court, was "damaged as a competitive force" even though at the time of the suit in 1961 it was making money and selling nearly twice as many pies as its nearest competitor—one of the big three. To the Court it was enough that Utah Pie's profits and sales were not as great as they might have been without the price war. The Utah decision makes price cutting by large firm riskier than ever, for they have to face the specter of damage suits by small firms who can claim damages if price competition threatens to hurt sales or profits, the Forgotten Man notwithstanding.

Still another devious pricing practice in the FTC mentality is "predatory" or "cut-throat" pricing. This

---

[1]386 U.S. 685 (1967).

pricing crime was charged against the Great Atlantic & Pacific Tea Company, a pioneer in low-cost groceries. In the A & P case, Robinson-Patman provisions impelled the A & P to seek ways and means of satisfying the price discrimination law and yet continue its basic policy of buying cheap and selling cheap. After 1936 the A & P purchase policy called upon suppliers to reduce their price rather than give credit for brokerage services. The FTC objected to the practice and was sustained by the court of appeals. The A & P then adopted a policy of direct purchase, avoiding all who sold through brokers. At this point the Antitrust Division took over from the FTC, charging that some A & P stores practiced "predatory" pricing, that A & P sought to eliminate local competition.[1]

The chain, for its part, fought its case to quite an extent in the nation's press, thereby enlisting to its cause millions of its distaff customers. In the end the company was found guilty and signed a rather mild consent decree in January 1954, agreeing in the main not to practice "predatory" purchasing and pricing, a variation on the theme of when-did-you-stop-beating-your-wife. But even the judge convicting the big food chain was forced to admit that "to buy, sell, and distribute to a substantial portion of 130 million people one and three-quarters billion dollars worth of food annually at a profit of $1\frac{1}{4}$ cents on each dollar is an achieve-

---

[1]*U.S.* v. *A & P,* 67F Supp. 626, affirmed 173 F. (2d) 79 (1949); and *A & P* v. *FTC,* 106 F. (2d) 667 (1939).

ment one may well be proud of."[1] Achievement or not, many states continue to slap discriminatory taxes on chain stores, in the ongoing undeclared war between the government and the Forgotten Man.

Perhaps the crowning achievement of the FTC's war on discriminatory pricing is the *Sun Oil* case, a case abounding in confusion and official cross-purposes.[2] It all began in 1955 when Gilbert McLean, a Sun dealer in Jacksonville, Florida, let the company know that he had been engaged in a price war by a nearby Super Test dealer—an independent brand service station. Sun was of course conscious of the fact that Robinson-Patman specifically authorized a seller to reduce his price "in good faith to meet an equally low price of a competitor." In addition, Sun Oil had in its possession a series of letters from the director of the FTC's Bureau of Investigation in which the director said that a seller is within his legal rights "in confining his price reductions to dealers in the vicinity of a dealer or dealers whose competition he seeks to meet, even though such action results in injury to customers to whom similar reductions are not made available." Sun thereupon granted price relief to McLean to enable him to match prices with the Super Test station.

When Sun's other franchised dealers in the area re-

---

[1]Consent decree, January 19, 1954, Commerce Clearing House, *Trade Reports,* 67, 658.
[2]*FTC* v. *Sun Oil Co.,* 371 U.S. 505 (1963). See also M. R. Lefkoe, "The Strange Case of Sun Oil," *Fortune,* August 1963.

quested similar price relief, Sun rejected the requests
and this brought on the dealers' complaint to the FTC.
The commission in turn charged Sun with discriminatory pricing, specifically with violation of Section 2(a)
of the Robinson-Patman Act, whereupon Sun asserted
Section 2(b) of the act—the "good faith" clause.

In rebuttal the FTC argued that Sun had not sought
to meet a price reduction of one of its own competitors
—another bulk supplier—but rather met a price reduction of a dealer's competitor—a competing gas station.
Sun appealed the FTC's cease and desist order to a
lower court and won its case there. The unanimous ruling of the Fifth Circuit Court of Appeals held that the
FTC

> denies the realities of the marketplace in refus-
> ing to accept the undeniable fact that a supplier
> of gasoline competes with a supplier-retailer at
> the consumer level through filling station oper-
> ators; tends to spread rather than localize price
> wars; and makes it impossible, as a practical
> matter, for a supplier to defend one of its filling
> stations, fighting for survival, or even to defend
> itself against destructive price raids of a sup-
> plier-retailer.

But the FTC took the case to the Supreme Court and
convinced it that Sun's "good faith" defense was lacking. The High Court based its reversal of the lower
court ruling on two assumptions—"that Super Test was
engaged solely in retail operations . . . [and that] Super

Test was not the beneficiary of any enabling price cut from its own supplier." Following these assumptions a footnote conceded:

> Were it otherwise, i.e., if it had appeared that either Super Test were an integrated supplier-retailer, or that it had received a price cut from its own supplier—presumably a competitor of Sun—we would be presented with a different case, as to which we herein neither express nor intimate any opinion.

So Sun Oil renewed the case in a lower court, supplying affidavits and other evidence showing Super Test to be indeed a supplier-retailer, owning, operating, and oftentimes supplying its chain of over sixty gas stations. In addition, Super Test got much of its gasoline supply from Orange State Oil, at the time an affiliate of Cities Service—i.e., one of Sun's direct competitors.

At any rate, the range of decisions offered here from Goodyear to Sun suggests that the range of regulatory authority of the Federal Trade Commission is extraordinarily broad, complex, and highly interventionistic. Robinson-Patman, for example, when it precludes lower so-called "discriminatory" prices, practically forces companies to engage in price discrimination—that is, forces sellers to charge some buyers what amount to higher discriminatory or noncompetitive prices—a result opposite to the presumed intention of the act.

As Princeton political scientist and university president, Woodrow Wilson, who did much to create the FTC in 1914, said in 1908:

> Regulation by commission is not regulation by
> law, but control according to the discretion of
> government officials. . . . Such methods of regu-
> lation, it may safely be predicted, will sooner or
> later by completely discredited by experience.

Thus did Dr. Wilson in effect speak well of market
self-regulation or, at most, governmental benign regulation. But Dr. Wilson clearly was not reckoning with
President Wilson.

There is little doubt that, as noted, self-regulation of
the market system is not perfect. Certainly competition
can be cumbersome; it can be heartless, striking down
small and occasionally big businesses—the streetcar companies earlier in this century, for example. The market
can give rise to temporary monopolies and consumer
deception, but it is still policed by the courts and by the
more powerful consumer.

In this vein, Philip Elman, a veteran of thirty-one
years in the federal government and a federal trade
commissioner, on his retirement called for radical struc-
tural reform of the Fourth Branch. He held that the
FTC and other so-called independent agencies were
independent from all but the interests they regulated.
He held further that the upshot was that the consumer
"suffers too much from the wrong kind of regulation."
He condemned the combination of the prosecutorial
and judicial functions in a single agency as making the
outcome of an FTC or any other agency proceeding
"a foregone conclusion."[1]

---

[1]Philip Elman, speech, St. Louis, Mo., August 11, 1970.

The Federal Trade Commission and the Robinson-Patman Acts in practice work out to be anticonsumer and should be repealed. The antitrust authority of the FTC should be transferred to the Antitrust Division; and its trade regulation function prohibiting outright deception and fraud should be transferred to the courts.

CHAPTER V

The Working Man and the National Labor Relations Board

I thought we were doing the right thing but I
certainly didn't mean to sink the ship.
>   —Chorus girl striker, a member
>   of the American Guild of Variety
>   Artists, picketing New York's
>   Latin Quarter and just learning
>   that the nightclub was closing
>   down, unable to meet both its
>   debts and the union's demands.
>   *New York Post,* February 20, 1969

The official overseer of collective bargaining in the
nation, the National Labor Relations Board, headquartered at 1717 Pennsylvania Avenue, N.W., Washington,
D.C., testifies eloquently to the high purpose of the
Washington way: After all, the NLRB ministers not to
plutocratic capital, but to the underdog, the democratic

trade union movement, to blue-collar working people and to their just and legitimate aspirations in American society.

The Labor Board is the regulatory agency empowered to administer the Wagner or National Labor Relations Act, as amended, a law which declares (Section 1):

> It is hereby declared to be the policy of the United States to eliminate the causes of certain substantial obstructions to the free flow of commerce and to mitigate and eliminate these obstructions when they have occurred by encouraging the practice and procedure of collective bargaining, and, by protecting the exercise by workers of full freedom of association, self-organization, and designation of representatives of their own choosing, for the purpose of negotiating the terms and conditions of their employment or other mutual aid or protection.

Of course, the NLRB, although nominally "independent," is also a political body, its five members appointed by the President, with the advice and consent of the Senate, for terms of five years each. Naturally, each appointment is also subject to hawk-like scrutiny by the Chamber of Commerce, NAM, and hordes of other industry and commerce groups in Washington on the one hand, and, on the other, by the labor chieftains of the AFL-CIO, the Railroad Brotherhoods, the Teamsters, the Hod Carriers, and hordes of other labor groups mostly headquartered—not by coincidence—in Washington.

The Herculean job of the NLRB is somehow to carry out the shifting and not always synchronized desires of Congress and the equally variegated desires of diverse pressure groups. Consider, for instance, the act's provisions on protecting "full" freedom of association. One provision outlaws the "yellow-dog" contract, in which the employee agrees not to join or remain in a union as a condition of employment. This provision forbids an employer from restraining or coercing his employees in any way in their right to organize and bargain collectively. But the provision also protects employees in their concomitant right to refrain from any and all such activity except—and this is quite an exception—under a perfectly legal compulsory union shop.

The union shop provision—a requirement that any nonunion employee must join the union (or at least pay dues to it) or forfeit his job—amounts to an interesting exercise in doublethink. For if a worker believes in the act's "full freedom of association" and chooses not to associate with the union (a "free-rider" in the union vernacular), then under the union shop the employer at the behest of the union must dismiss him forthwith. Without the union shop, however, unions argue they would be "burdened" by representing nonunion, non-dues-paying, "free-riding" employees. The union shop, however, would be perfectly fine in a really free society. Thus if an employer and union wish to see all employees as members of the union, they should have the right to make such a contract, and employees and prospective employees not liking the idea of union membership should be free to quit or not apply for employment under such a condition.

But in terms of labor law our society is not entirely free. If any employer insists that only nonunion employees be employed, he is forbidden from doing so by the provision against yellow-dog contracts. Yet yellow-dog, like the union shop, is also freedom of contract, and AFL-CIO President George Meany has been fond of defending union shop clauses precisely on this score of freedom. But apart from the one-way feature of this argument, the rub with the union shop in practice is that it is rarely adopted voluntarily by an employer; rather, the employer usually gets a demand to adopt a union shop clause in the labor agreement or be subjected to pressure—strikes, picketing, exhortation, excoriation, secondary boycotts or other persuaders in the union arsenal.

To be sure, there is still a concession to the individual employee's right to freedom of association. This is the much contested Section 14(b) of the Taft-Hartley Amendment to the National Labor Relations Act, reading:

> Nothing in this Act shall be construed as authorizing the execution or application of agreements requiring membership in a labor organization as a condition of employment in any State or Territory in which such execution or application is prohibited by State or Territorial Law.

So acting under what amounts to a congressional invitation, some nineteen states have passed laws guaranteeing freedom of choice to join or not to join a union in order to keep a job; these are the so-called "right-to-work" laws—laws which in effect Congress has given and which Congress can take away. And that was precisely what President Johnson called on Congress to do —repeal 14(b), a key defense of voluntary unionism. Yet voluntary unionism meets the tenets of a free society and the freedom of association specifically provided in the Wagner Act.

Compulsory unionism, on the other hand, not only limits such freedom but it can breed corruption. For example, Sylvester Petro, professor of law at New York University and a former union organizer, described in detail the abuses of union power uncovered in the late 1950s before the McClellan Committee of the Senate, arguing:[1]

> The McClellan record reveals . . . that compulsory unionism is the principal cause of corruption and maladministration of unions; it draws into unions the kind of men who abuse union members, and takes from the members any real power to rid themselves of the looters.

Here are some of the guarded findings of the McClellan Committee on industrial life under the National Labor Relations Act in its report in 1958:[2]

> There has been a significant lack of democratic procedures in the unions studied.
> The international unions surveyed by the

---

[1]Sylvester Petro, *Power Unlimited,* Ronald, 1959, p. 287.
[2]Senate Report 1417, 85th Congress, 2nd Session.

committee have flagrantly abused their power
to place local unions under trusteeship or
supervisorship.

Certain managements have extensively
engaged in collusion with unions.

There has been widespread misuse of funds
in the unions studied.

Violence in labor-management disputes, widely
regarded as a relic of the organizing era of the
Thirties, still exists to an extent where it
may be justifiably labeled a crime against the
community.

Certain managements and their agents have
engaged in a number of illegal and improper
activities in violation of the National Labor
Relations Act, as amended in 1947 (the
Taft-Hartley law).

The weapon of organizational picketing has
been abused by some of the unions studied.

Gangsters and hoodlums have successfully
infiltrated some labor unions, sometimes at
high levels.

An extensive "no-man's land" in Federal-state
jurisdiction has been uncovered by committee
testimony.

Law-enforcement officers have been lax in
investigating and prosecuting acts of violence
resulting from labor-management disputes.

Members of the legal profession have played a
dubious role in their relationships with
officials of some unions.

Another interesting side of the National Labor Relations Act is its tacit and inadvertent reinforcement of a low-key class war between "labor" and "management" (or, in the language of old-line unionists, "capital"). For example, the act tells the employer not to dominate or interfere with the formation of any union—or contribute financial or any other kind of support to it. Of course, the theory is that employer financial support would subvert the effectiveness of the union in securing gains from the employer, that the support would, bluntly, amount to a bribe.

But this theory presupposes the general effectiveness of unionism to boost real wages and protect job opportunities. This supposition, however, cannot be simply assumed. If unions are viewed only in terms of their effect on the economy, according to Princeton University's Professor Albert Rees, they must be considered "an obstacle to the optimum performance of our economic system." Unions, he says, alter[1]

the wage structure in a way that impedes the growth of employment in sectors of the economy where productivity and income are naturally high and that leaves too much labor in low-income sectors of the economy like southern agriculture and the least skilled service trades. It benefits most those workers who

---

[1]Albert Rees, *The Economics of Trade Unions,* University of Chicago, 1962, pp. 194–195. See also H. Gregg Lewis, *Unionism and Relative Wages in the United States,* University of Chicago, 1963.

would in any case be relatively well off, and while some of this gain may be at the expense of the owners of capital, most of it must be at the expense of consumers and the lower-paid workers. Unions interfere blatantly with the use of the most productive techniques in some industries, and this effect is probably not offset by the stimulus to higher productivity furnished by some other unions.

Yet in view of the Wagner Act, Congress and the NLRB seem to be in something of a fog as to the source of wage improvement and job opportunities. Certainly it is not twisting the arm of the employer with strikes, slowdowns, picketing, featherbedding, secondary boycotts, and the like. Nor is it a matter of slowing down automation or asking Congress and state legislatures for higher and higher minimum wages and unemployment compensation payments—all of which can work to increase inflation and/or unemployment, and lower real wages.

Take the case of minimum wages, even if it is not the direct concern of the NLRB. The first legal minimum wage was fixed at 25¢ an hour in 1938. By 1956 it had reached $1.00 and by 1968 it reached $1.60 an hour. The jump between 1955 and 1968 was 114 percent for minimum wages while during the same period average hourly wages in manufacturing increased only by about half that percentage.

A result has been that while shortages have developed

for skilled labor, the proportion of unemployed among the unskilled, among teen-agers and nonwhites has grown. The outstanding victim has been the Negro teen-ager. In 1952 the unemployment rate among white and nonwhite teen-agers was the same—9 percent. By 1968, the unemployment rate among white teen-agers was 11.6 percent, but among nonwhite teen-agers it reach 26.6 percent. Thus, minimum wage laws, like our trade union legislation, have contributed to unemployment or inflation or, as in 1970–1971 a combination of the two.

In any event, national real wage improvement and job opportunities stem mainly from increased worker efficiency, from capital investment in the tools of production, from entrepreneurs scouting and filling consumer demand at prices consumers want to pay, from the whole process known as the free enterprise system.

Still another interesting side of the National Labor Relations Act lies in its directive to the employer that he cannot discriminate in his hiring, firing, and advancement policies because of the union activity of an employee. This raises an interesting dilemma: Just how does the NLRB detect and measure discrimination? Can, for example, the NLRB or its trial examiner probe the inner recesses of the employer's mind when, say, he passes over an aggressive shop steward in handing out promotions? Charges and countercharges, grievances and counter-grievances, in such situations can and do arise, creating plant dissension and unrest, along with strained union-management relations, possibly including the filing of an unfair labor practice charge with the NLRB.

Also, the act declares that an employer commits an unfair labor practice when he refuses to bargain in "good faith" with union officials certified by the NLRB as representing his employees. But like "discrimination," "good faith" is difficult to ascertain and measure and therefore makes for union-management rancor and litigation. To be sure, unions and their officials—under the Taft-Hartley Act—are also prohibited from committing "unfair labor practices," prohibitions omitted from the Wagner Act. For example, unions are prohibited from charging "excessive or discriminatory" initation fees. Moreover, they are prohibited from securing wages from employers for "services not performed or not to be performed." In other words, featherbedding and make-work practices are prohibited—or were so under the original intent of Congress.

This latter prohibition, however, doesn't reckon with the ingenuity of the Washington way—or, more strictly, with the ingenuity of members of the Labor Board—to work around legislative intent. So some union printers, despite the fact that their employers have preset printed mats, continue to set "bogus type" (type which never sees the black of ink), and firemen, whose jobs are holdovers from the days of coal-stoked steam engines, continue to stare out of the cab windows of Diesel locomotives which engineers guide down the tracks. Featherbedding? Hardly. These are "services performed," and certainly paid for, but, in the end, paid for in higher prices by the consumer.

How did the National Labor Relations Act and other labor legislation come to pass? A major impetus can be traced back to passage of the Clayton Act in 1914, an act hailed by the trade unions of the day as labor's Magna Carta: The act exempted unions from the antimonopoly provisions of the Sherman Act, which earlier had ensnared the Hatters Union for antitrust violation and promised to ensnare others. Further, the act put forth the ringing declaration (Section 6) that "the labor of a human being is not an article or commodity of commerce." The declaration, however, departs from supply and demand theory, and observable economic data—e.g., the income differential between the ditchdigger and the brain surgeon. Even centuries ago a cagey commentator in England wisely noted that when two masters chased after one journeyman, the journeyman's wages tended to rise; conversely, when two journeymen chased after one master, the journeymen's wages tended to fall.

At any rate, the Clayton Act historically broke the dam of legislative resistance to union protectionism, and the ensuing flood of labor legislation transformed the trade union movement from a voluntary competitive movement into one possessed with monopoly powers— a movement today embracing more than 20 million members out of a civilian labor force of some 84 million. After the Clayton Act came a deluge of federal labor paternalism and interventionism: The Railway Labor Act of 1926, which required railroads to bargain collectively with the railroad brotherhoods; the Norris-LaGuardia Anti-Injunction Act of 1932, which practically prevented use of federal injunctions against unions in labor disputes and rendered yellow-dog contracts unenforceable in federal courts; and the Wagner Act of 1935.

The NLRB-creating Wagner Act was built upon the labor provisions of the National Industrial Recovery Act of 1933, which had been declared unconstitutional by the Supreme Court. The Wagner Act helped spawn the Congress of Industrial Organizations. At first the CIO, originally known as the Committee for Industrial Organization, was a division of the American Federation of Labor—essentially a federation of craft unions. The CIO was expelled in 1937 from the parent organization and renamed the Congress of Industrial Organizations with John L. Lewis as its first president. With the backing of the industrial union-minded NLRB, the CIO bowled over whole industries in its mighty organization drive—autos, steel, chemicals, rubber, electrical manufacturing, communications, textiles, meat-packing. So the new labor law served to boost labor union membership as never before. Labor Department estimates place the boost from about 3.7 million in 1935 to about 10.5 million in 1941, with a further lift during the Second World War to 14.8 million in 1945, to the 20 million-plus of today.

Following the Wagner Act came still more legislation to "protect" the workingman: the Walsh-Healey Government Contracts Act of 1936, which set minimum wages and maximum hours in firms with federal contracts; the Byrnes Strike-Breaker Act of 1936, which prohibited employers from transporting across state lines persons engaged in strike-breaking activities; the Merchant Marine Act of 1936, which required American ships to hire American seamen for not less than three-fourths of their crews and set minimum wages and maximum hours for all American ships getting Treasury subsidies. The idea of federally-set minimum wages and maximum hours was extended from public contractors and ship operators to virtually all American industry when Congress passed the Fair Labor Standards Act of 1938.

After World War II the pendulum swung against the unions, but not very far: In 1947 came the aforementioned Taft-Hartley Act (the "slave labor act," according to trade union officialdom); and in 1959 the Landrum-Griffin or Labor Management Reporting and Disclosure Act, which required unions and managements to submit periodic reports to the Department of Labor. The Taft-Hartley and Landrum-Griffin laws were passed after long and heated lobbying, involved parliamentary maneuvering, and, in the case of Taft-Hartley, a presidential veto.

So, in legislative sum, the federal government sought to improve, in one way or another, the lot of the workingman by administrative intervention and legislative fiat—by governmental price-fixing rules and regulations on wages and hours, by the adjudicating powers of the NLRB, and by government-conferred privileges and antitrust exemptions for trade unions. The result is what Sumner Slichter of Harvard called a "laboristic society," and an official two-facedness on competition that recalls a passage from *Alice in Wonderland:*

> "When *I* use a word," said Humpty Dumpty to Alice in a scornful tone, "it means just what I choose it to mean—neither more nor less."
> "The question is," replied Alice, "whether you can make words mean so many different things."

Thus, officially, as seen in the discussion on antitrust and the FTC, competition is considered good and monopoly bad in business dealings in goods and services—save in one type of services—labor. For labor services, competition is considered bad and monopoly good. Trade unions can legally do almost the same things that for business firms are forbidden. Unions are allowed and indeed encouraged to monopolize regional, industry, or occupational job markets, to get together and fix job prices for crafts and whole industries—and, if need be, to shut down whole industries by industry-wide strikes.

In addition, unions are permitted, as previously noted, to require unwilling employees to accept membership or lose their jobs and to compel employers to negotiate for all employees in an NLRB-designated bargaining unit, including those who want no union or some other union. Moreover, trade unions appear to get a good deal of immunity from local prosecution in the use of coercion and even overt violence in strikes, picketing, and secondary boycotts. The police, in other words, all too often look the other way.

Yet this double standard for labor and management goes to still greater lengths. Unions, for example, enjoy substantial immunity from injunctions by federal courts, thanks, as noted, to the Norris-LaGuardia Act. Too, unions can use union funds for purposes beyond collective bargaining, including politics (though not in the form of direct contributions), even when union membership dues payments are required of all workers, who may or may not be willing union members. Again, unions have exemption from income taxation and frequently can avoid liability for personal or property damage to employers or to others by union members involved in union activities such as strikes and picketing.

Ironically this double standard supposedly implements the Wagner Act's aim of easing the "free flow of commerce." But the Wagner Act was immediately followed by an unexpected long and hard reign of strikes and occasional violence continuing down to the present. Even the New Deal strategists had not anticipated the ferocity and radicalism of the auto sitdown strikes, the open warfare between the organized and unorganized in the coal fields, the Memorial Day massacre at Republic Steel's Chicago mill in 1937, the appearance of Communist elements in the labor movement (which receded with the Nazi-Soviet nonaggression pact of 1939). National strikes occurred again and again in railroads, telephones, steel, coal, and shipping, producing all manner of reactions. In 1946 President Truman, for example, threatened to draft railroad strikers into the Army.

To cite another example: over the years the shipping

industry, a very sick industry despite heavy subsidies, has circumvented part of the high cost of American unionism by deploying American-owned ships to foreign construction and to foreign flags, especially the flags of Panama, Liberia, and Honduras, in order to avail itself of foreign wages. But even this escape hatch was challenged by the NLRB. In the *United Fruit* case[1] the NLRB backed the National Maritime Union when the union sought certification as the collective bargaining representative of foreign seamen employed by a fleet of Honduran flag vessels owned by United Fruit. The Supreme Court, however, held that the board's jurisdiction did not extend to other nations and other nationals.

The NLRB has even challenged the right of free speech as guaranteed in the First Amendment. In *NLRB* v. *Virginia Electric & Power Co.*,[2] the Supreme Court in 1941 seemed to have delimited the First Amendment when it said that an employer was constitutionally protected in expressing his viewpoint on labor matters as long as his statements did not amount to "coercion." As a practical matter, however, the NLRB was disposed to find employer statements made just before NLRB representation elections rife with implied "coercion," and as a result most employers simply clammed up. The upshot in 1947 was the inclusion in Taft-Hartley of Section 8(c) which guaranteed free speech as follows:

---

[1] 134 NLRB 287.
[2] 314 U.S. 469.

The expressing of any views, argument or opinion, or the dissemination thereof, whether in written, printed, graphic, or visual form, shall not constitute or be evidence of an unfair labor practice under any of the provisions of this Act, if such expression contains no threat of reprisal or force or promise of benefit.

This is certainly clear and forthright. Notwithstanding, the Labor Board administrators of administrative law have not been necesarily inconvenienced by such reaffirmation of the First Amendment. In the *May Department Stores* case,[1] for example, the NLRB held that an employer before an election could not speak out to his employees against the union on company time and property unless the union was given the same opportunity. This decision has become known as the "equal opportunity" doctrine. Still, the equality seems to be one-sided. The board did not say the employer ought to have equal time on union property or equal space in the union paper.

To trace the evolution of the "equal opportunity" doctrine, let us look into this case more fully. To begin with, the May Company was operating under a legally established rule against employee solicitation by unions in its two stores in the Cleveland area. Just before a representation election, however, the employer made a number of talks critical of the union to employee groups

---

[1] 136 NLRB 71, 49 LRRM 1862.

on company time and property. None of the speeches carried any promise of benefit or threat of reprisal. The union asked for an equal opportunity to address store employees. The request was rejected and the union subsequently lost the election.

The board, however, set aside the election on grounds of an unfair labor practice on the part of the company, with the board majority finding a "glaring imbalance" in the employer's use of company time and property while the union had but "catch-as-catch-can" methods such as meetings on employees' time and contacts via mail, phone, newspapers, and home visits. Board member Philip Ray Rodgers dissented from the majority, citing the freedom of speech guaranteed in the First Amendment, and also in Section 8(c) of the Taft-Hartley Law. The Sixth Circuit Court of Appeals reversed the NLRB decision and upheld the view of dissenting board member Rodgers.

Yet the attitude of the NLRB to the right of free speech continues. In 1964, by a four to one vote, the board held that General Electric did not bargain "in good faith" in its 1960 contract negotiations with the International Union of Electrical, Radio and Machine Workers, AFL-CIO. Said the board:[1]

> It is inconsistent . . . for an employer to mount a campaign, as Respondent [GE] did, both before and during negotiations, for the purpose of disparaging and discrediting the statutory rep-

---

[1]150 NLRB 192.

resentative in the eyes of its employee constituents, to seek to persuade the employees to
exert pressure on the representative to submit to
the will of the employer, and to create the impression that the employer rather than the
union is the true protector of the employees'
interests. As the Trial Examiner phrased it, the
employer's statutory obligation is to deal with
the employees through the union, and not with
the union through the employees.

The board then goes on to accuse GE of communi-
cating its position directly to its employees, a GE policy
that has become known as "Boulewarism" after its retired vice president, Lemuel R. Bouleware. Yet the
union, the IUE, communicated its position directly to
its GE members. The principle of the NLRB, apparently, is that the employer must simply trust the union
to outline accurately the employer's profit picture, his
competitive situation, the size of his offer in terms of
wages, hours, and benefits. But the fact is that union
officers and the union press have at times been known
to stretch the truth, as indeed have company executives
and house organs. Still, employees should be able to
hear both sides, and both sides should have the opportunity to present their sides, or so fair play would appear
to dictate—but not, apparently, to the NLRB.
The NLRB decision in *Darlington Mills-Deering
Milliken*[1] seems to have jarred the Bill of Rights a bit

---

[1] 139 NLRB 241.

more, in particular the Fifth Amendment affirming due process in matters of life, liberty and property. Specifically, the decision serves notice on employers that they cannot simply shut down a plant involved in a labor dispute, even if it is uneconomical, despite all the traditional rights of private property. So *Darlington* sets quite a precedent. What started it?

In 1956 the Textile Workers Union of America began an organizing drive to unionize the workers of the Darlington Company, a South Carolina textile mill. Controlling interest in the company—some two-thirds—was held by the Milliken family which also controlled the Deering-Milliken companies. Darlington had been for a number of years a marginal operation. Nonetheless, the union organizers mesmerized the workers with dreams of fatter pay envelopes at the expense of fat company profits—profits which the owners described as phantom. In any event, the Textile Workers won a representation election on September 7, 1956. Confronted with the dilemma of insistent demands for greater wages with little or no likelihood for improved productivity in a fiercely competitive industry, the Darlington owners shut down the mill, and on December 13, 1956, the buildings were sold at public auction.

The shutdown rattled the TWUA's southern organizers, especially as textile manufacturers peppered the southern textile belt with bumper stickers that warned "Remember Darlington." Meanwhile, seeing their jobs evaporate before their eyes, 83 percent of the workers signed a petition saying they would rather forget the union, but it was too late as far as the company was concerned. The NLRB entered the case when the TWUA filed charges of unfair labor practices against the company.

In hearings before the board, the company said it had acted out of economic necessity and not out of anti-union vindictiveness. Further, it maintained it had the right to shut down the mill and liquidate it. The NLRB, in a three-to-two decision, held that such a right is superseded when it conflicts with existing labor law. The board argued that Darlington bargained in "bad faith" and that existing law

> literally proscribes Darlington's closing of its business in retaliation for the employees' selection of the union as their bargaining representative . . . Darlington's threat to close its mills if the union became the bargaining representative is a classical example of a violation.

The NLRB charge of "bad faith" against Darlington illustrates the difficulty of protecting the rights of freedom of speech for employers and freedom of organization for employees as both freedoms are construed by the NLRB. Taft-Hartley, as noted, expressly permits employers free speech but includes the proviso that such speech should be restrained from any "threat" of economic reprisal for union activity.

Yet if the mill owners believed union organization would prove to be the straw that would break the Darlington back, can they be prevented from expressing such a belief and still be permitted freedom of speech? Can a statement of an unpleasant fact or unpleasant opinion in collective bargaining be construed to be a "threat" to employees? Indeed, could not management be charged with "bad faith" for not warning employees that excessive wage demands could in fact jeopardize their jobs?

When the Supreme Court upheld the NLRB in the *Darlington* case in 1965[1] it maintained the right of an employer to "terminate his entire business for any reason he pleases," but added that

> a partial closing is an unfair labor practice if motivated by a purpose to chill unionism in any of the remaining plants of the single employer and if the employer may reasonably have foreseen that such closing will likely have that effect.

As for Darlington, the Court ordered the NLRB to further probe the purpose and effect of the plant closing on the company's other employees. But the *Darlington* case—still not settled after fifteen years of litigation—is only one case among thousands.

A recent annual report of the NLRB bespeaks great activity, including:

---

[1] 380 U.S. 263.

More than 30,400 cases of all kinds were received, of which 17,040 were unfair labor practice charges. The others were representation petitions and related matters.

Cases closed were 29,500, of which a record 16,400 involved unfair labor practice charges.

The board issued a total of 1,023 unfair labor practice decisions.

The General Counsel's office issued 1,945 formal complaints.

More than a half million employees cast ballots in NLRB-conducted elections.

And so it goes, thousands of cases each year as the board perseveres in its fourth decade of seeking to adjudicate the nation's union-management relations. The NLRB is a quixotic regulatory agency, trying to reconcile the apparently irreconcilable, trying to protect the employee's right to join a union but largely unable to protect the individual employee's concomitant right not to join, trying to free the flow of commerce while encouraging the incentive to strike, trying to achieve peaceful bargaining but having great difficulty distinguishing between bargaining in "good faith" and in "bad faith," trying to uphold free speech while preventing employers from fully telling their side.

Voluntary unionism should be an integral part of a free society—and the goal of public policy. Current unionism, based largely upon compulsion and monopo-

ly, is an anachronism left over from the Great Depression. It has greatly contributed to, depending on the
stage of the business cycle, unemployment, inflation, or
both. Compulsory unionism, along with the National
Labor Relations Board, should be phased out of existence, with the courts taking over many of the board's
adjudicating functions.

CHAPTER VI

Transportation and the Interstate Commerce Commission

The free market is a decentralized regulator of our economic system. The free market is not only a more efficient decision maker than even the wisest planning body, but even more important, the free market keeps economic power widely dispersed. It thus is a vital underpinning of our democratic system.

—President John F. Kennedy
September 26, 1962

In March 1963 President Kennedy pressed Congress for action on his transportation program, which heretically called for removal of Interstate Commerce Commission regulatory authority over certain minimum freight rates. Said the President, in the typical two-sided language of the Washington way, hailing competition on one hand and decrying "destructive competition" on the other:

> The law should provide . . . equality of opportunity for all modes and for all passengers and shippers, without any special preferences. There should be maximum reliance on the forces of competition consistent with a continuing need for protection against destructive competition between forms of transportation or between competing carriers.

But even such mild deregulation did not sit well with powerful forces in the transportation industry. For example, the barge interests—formally known in Washington as the American Waterways Operators—were stunned, charging the President with allowing "well-financed" railroads to be "free to pick and choose their competition and kill at will."[1] The American Trucking Association was not happy either, as may be inferred from the following editorial in the April 1963 issue of *Fleet Owner,* a monthly trade organ for the trucking industry:

> The Administration's willingness to listen to compromise proposals stems from soundings in Congress indicating that its deregulation proposal probably couldn't be passed in its present form. The trucking industry, which bitterly opposes it because it would mainly benefit the

---

[1]*Business Week,* April 14, 1962.

railroads, is making its influence felt in Congress. In addition, the industry has brought pressure on the White House. Some Administration officials claim it was "the truck lobby" which succeeded at the White House level in delaying submission of this year's legislation to Congress for two weeks in an effort to water down the President's main proposal. Although Kennedy repeated to Congress his preference for deregulation, he expressed a slightly more hospitable view than last year toward his second choice of broadening regulation to cover bulk and farm goods. This was a concession to trucker pressure.

Trucker pressure indeed. The history of transport regulation in America is a history of pressure, both before and after passage of the Interstate Commerce Act —pressure by transporters and transport users and their many friends in and out of government, by Congress, the courts, and the executive branch and once the act became law, by the ICC itself.

Federal participation in railroading began innocuously enough as laws granting rights of way through public lands and remission of duties on imported railway equipment and construction materials. But once started, this mild intervention worked up to vast land grants, first to the Illinois Central and the Mobile and Ohio Railroads in 1850. In all, 155,504,944 acres of public lands were granted to the railroads, according to Donaldson's *Public Lands* published in 1884, of

which 131,350,534 were actually taken. William R.
King, senator from Alabama and later Vice-President
of the United States under President Pierce, defended
the grants in the Senate:[1]

> We are met by the objection that this is an im-
> mense grant—that it is a great quantity of land.
> Well, sir, it is a great quantity; but it will be
> there for 500 years; and unless some mode of
> the kind proposed be adopted, it will never
> command ten cents.

Even so, as it turned out, the government-encouraged
railroad boom also brought severe problems in its wake
—to name two: an uneconomic build-up of railroad
capacity and a misallocation of routes. In the 1850s
alone more than twenty thousand miles of railroads
were constructed. In 1869 the Union Pacific and Central Pacific completed the transcontinental link at Pro-
montory Point, Utah, but soon there was a second,
third, and even a fourth link, aside from north-south
links. The land-grant railroad boom, generating over-
capacity, misrouting, and other malinvestment, unquestionably helped to produce the depression of 1873, in
which railroad profits all but disappeared, tracks rusted,
and the weaker railroads plunged into bankruptcy.

The depression brought further problems. For one
thing, further federal and state intervention in railroad
affairs was foreshadowed by the rise of the Grangers,

---

[1]Stewart H. Holbrook, *The Story of American Railroads,* Crown,
1947, p. 157.

those sturdy Patrons of Husbandry who quickly discovered that lobbying at the statehouse and in Congress would not go unnoticed. In 1872 some thirteen hundred local granges had been organized. Two years later, with the depression of 1873 knocking farm prices sharply down, more than twenty thousand granges were in existence, clamoring for an end to rural inequity and discrimination at the hands of greedy railroad tycoons, merciless farm equipment cartels, vicious warehouse operators, and bloated eastern capitalists generally. The tenor of the complaints can be surmised from the grand master's call for public control over the "monopolistic" railroads to the annual meeting of the National Grange in 1874:[1]

> When we plant a crop we can only guess what it will cost to send it to market, for we are the slaves of those whom we created . . . In our inmost soul we feel deeply wronged at the return made for the kind and liberal spirit we have shown them.

Such pressure, not surprisingly, yielded results. States such as Iowa, Illinois, Minnesota, and Wisconsin passed restrictive legislation against the railroad and warehouse "monopolies," so that henceforward they would be treated strictly as public utilities in which their services were specified and their rates were fixed—the very essence of ICC philosophy.

---

[1]*Proceedings,* National Grange of the Patrons of Husbandry, 1874, p. 14.

The key case manifesting and perpetuating this philosophy of interventionistic regulation was *Munn* v. *Illinois,* decided against Munn by the U.S. Supreme Court in 1877, a case which paved the way for the ICC. Plaintiff Munn, a Chicago grain-elevator operator, assailed the unassailable: government omnipotence and official Illinois acquiescence to Granger pressure demanding laws to "regulate" railroads and grain warehouse and elevator operators.

Chief Justice Waite and his colleagues were more than equal to Munn. The Chief Justice referred to the *Slaughterhouse* decision of the Court in 1873,[1] a case in which the Supreme Court maintained that the private property of a number of New Orleans butchers had not been taken without due process when Louisiana handed a twenty-five-year monopoly of all city slaughtering to a single slaughterhouse. Declared Chief Justice Waite ruling against Munn:[2]

> When, therefore, one devotes his property to a use in which the public has an interest, he, in effect, grants to the public an interest in that use, and must submit to be controlled by the public, for the common good, to the extent of the interest he has thus created.

Thanks in large measure to *Munn* v. *Illinois,* state Granger regulatory laws got on the books, and it was

---

[1]*Slaughterhouse Cases,* 16 Wall. 26 (1873).
[2]94 U.S. 113 (1877).

not long before a consumerist national Granger law—
the Interstate Commerce Act—took its place along with
state laws regulating commerce. A catalyst giving rise
to the Interstate Commerce Act was the Supreme Court
decision in *Wabash, St. Louis and Pacific Railway* v.
Illinois,[1] declaring that states could not regulate interstate railroads even though the national government
had not acted, thus bringing to a head the demand for
passage of a national Granger law.

The Grangers were but one headache for the railroads; the overexpansion of rail capacity was another.
Railroad managements sought refuge in overt and cov-
ert agreements allocating markets, fixing rates, pooling
profits, and granting secret and not-so-secret rebates,
negotiated rates, and various kinds of preferences to
shippers.

Such pooling agreements had disadvantages for the
would-be monopolists. In any pool there was frequently
if not inevitably the problem of a railroad management
ungentlemanly slipping out of a gentlemen's agreement,
openly or secretly, or another management fudging his
accounting "losses" or "profits," or still another staying
out of the pool entirely with a view toward undercutting
his rivals. Even if the pooling agreements were successful and all members lived up to their "responsibility,"
the resulting higher rates and profits tended to attract
other roads into undercutting competition, or into the
agreement. Either way, the original pool members saw

---

[1] 118 U.S. 557 (1886).

their business and profits dwindle in the finer split-up of the available business. Lastly, while pooling was not then illegal, it nonetheless was unenforceable as to contractual commitments. Welchers on the agreement could not be brought to heel in court under applicable common law. In short, combinations and conspiracies against trade may appeal to the monopolistic mentality, but in practice, unless enforced by government, they tend to evaporate.

So, even with widespread railroad pooling, rates worked downward, especially in highly competitive rail hub centers such as Chicago and New York. These centers acted as magnets for industry and commerce and the industrial geography of the country was thereby molded. Cities and regions with but one or two railroads felt disadvantaged and added to the swelling chorus of complaints against the railroads. Beside the Grange, Congress heard calls for railroad regulation from the Greenback Party, the Farmers Alliance, the Farmers Union, the Agricultural Wheel, the Brothers of Freedom, the Cooperative Union of America, the Farmers Mutual Benefit Association, and, perhaps most disturbing of all to railroad investors, the Populist Party. The Populists, who eventually claimed William Jennings Bryan as their champion, asked not for mere regulation of the railroads but for outright government ownership and operation.

Railroad magnates, quite naturally, were shaken by the political drift. The economic drift was none better. The Panic of 1884 dropped railroad security prices precipitously. Many railroads went into receivership.

Muckrakers, to add insult to injury, found their mark in the misadventures in railroad finance by tycoons Jay Gould, James Fisk, and Daniel Drew. Railroads turned increasingly to Congress for relief.

In March 1885 the U.S. Senate appointed a five-member select committee on interstate commerce, known as the Cullom Committee, "to investigate and report upon the subject of the regulation of transportation." The Cullom Report was released in 1886, and in it the committee complained of great railroad combinations, stock watering ("this practice has unquestionably done more to keep alive a popular feeling of hostility against the railroads of the United States than any other one cause"), unpublished rate making, and manifold discrimination against shippers, regions, and goods ("the paramount evil chargeable against the operation of the transportation systems of the United States, as now conducted, is unjust discrimination between persons, places, commodities, or particular descriptions of traffic").[1] The report, reflecting the philosophy of *Munn* v. *Illinois,* further contended railroads enjoyed private privileges and yet performed public functions, and were, therefore, quasi-public servants, very much subject to public control.

The report also took special note of the testimony of Colonel Albert Fink, vice-president of operations for the Louisville and Nashville Railroad and in 1877 organizer of the Trunk Line Association, a superpool ar-

---

[1]*Cf.,* Shelby M. Cullom, *Fifty Years of Public Service,* McClurg, 1911.

rangement designed, hopefully, to put an end to rate wars. In his testimony, Colonel Fink welcomed legalization and official enforcement of what had been private and woefully ineffectual pooling. Hence Colonel Fink's blunt request of the Cullom Committee: "Congress should legalize pooling, and impose a heavy penalty for any violation of the pooling agreement."[1] And when Senator Cullom inquired of Charles Francis Adams, President of the Union Pacific, how he would feel if Congress were to pass a law not only encouraging pooling but prohibiting pooling leaks such as rebates, an enthusiastic Adams replied:[2]

> It would be the greatest boon you could confer, because that would do away with the lack of confidence of which I just now spoke. If you could provide any way by which all passenger and freight agents could be absolutely debarred from making reductions from published rates, and from deceiving each other while doing it, you would be very much more successful than I have been in my limited sphere.

Thus did railroads request, openly and otherwise, federal assistance to reinforce wavering cartels, to save the railroads from the perils of unenforceable pooling and preclude the hazards of "cut-throat" competition.

The result of all this pressure on Congress, from the

---

[1] *Senate Report 46 (The Cullom Report)*, 1886, p. 117.
[2] *Ibid,* p. 1205.

railroads on one side and the Grangers and the Populists on the other, was to bring about passage of the Interstate Commerce Act in 1887. The act created a mighty regulatory precedent, the Interstate Commerce Commission, the first "independent" regulatory agency, and gave it the beginnings of far-reaching authority over transportation. To be sure, in its beginnings the ICC did not have the power to fix rates which most roads had wanted so badly. Rates, however, had to be published and adhered to without "any special rate, rebate, drawback, or other device," and without "any undue or unreasonable preference or advantage to any particular description of traffic." Pooling was forbidden but its rough equivalents of joint banking control and rate-fixing associations were, by implication, quite all right.

The ICC, once established, requested greater regulatory powers from Congress. With time and with railroad backing, the requests were granted, sympathetic regulatory power grew, for reasons well brought out in a clairvoyant letter from President Cleveland's Attorney General, Richard S. Olney, to railroad tycoon Charles E. Perkins, president of the Burlington and Quincy Railroad:[1]

> The Commission, as its functions have now
> been limited by the courts, is, or can be made,
> of great use to the railroads. It satisfies the

---

[1]Quoted in Matthew Josephson, *The Politicos,* Harcourt, Brace, 1938, p. 526.

popular clamor for Government supervision of
the railroads, at the same time that the supervision is almost entirely nominal. Further, the
older such a commission gets to be, the more
inclined it will be found to take the business
and railroad view of things. It thus becomes a
sort of barrier between the railroad corporations and the people and a sort of protection
against crude legislation hostile to railroad interests . . . The part of wisdom is not to destroy
the Commission, but to utilize it.

The commission was anything but destroyed; it was
indeed utilized, and the utilization brought on stronger
interventionistic legislation. The Elkins Act of 1903
plugged some loopholes, reinforcing the provisions
against railroad price-cutting in the form of rebates and
other "discriminatory" concessions to shippers. Cartelization was well on its way. Thoughtfully, Congress in
the Hepburn Act of 1906 granted the ICC jurisdiction
over express companies, sleeping-car companies, and oil
pipelines, thus beginning a long trend toward envelop-
ing into the ICC fold practically every potentially competitive mode of transportation.

Even more considerately, the ICC was also handed
its sought-for and most potent power to fix maximum
rates whenever it deemed railroad charges in individual
cases as unreasonable, and also the power to prescribe
through-routes and through-route maximum rates.
These two powers alone helped to subject the ICC—

already the agency in the middle—to even greater pressure: railroads naturally seeking to pull maximum rates higher, shippers naturally seeking to get them lower. Consider the power to determine through-routes: The ICC was apparently presumed able to anticipate market trends and population shifts and to forego political pressure from competing cities and railroads anxious for lucrative through-route business.

With time came additional acts, additional powers, additional pressures. The Mann-Elkins Act of 1910 permitted the ICC to pass upon proposed rate changes. The Panama Canal Act of 1912, designed to insure East Coast-West Coast traffic for the Canal, precluded railroad investments in competitive water carriers. The Valuation Act of 1913 instructed the ICC to evaluate railroad properties as a basis for decisions on rate levels. The Esch-Cummins Transportation Act of 1920 went further still, authorizing the ICC to fix all rates so as to yield a "fair return" and to prescribe something quite new and overtly anticonsumer: minimum rates. The act instructed the commission to price railroad services

> so that carriers as a whole (or as a whole in each of such rate groups or territories as the Commission may from time to time designate) will, under honest, efficient and economical management, earn an aggregate annual net railway operating income equal as nearly as may be, to a fair return upon the aggregate value of the railway property of such carriers held for and used in the service of transportation.

The "fair return" provision initially fixed at 5½ percent, later lifted to 5¾ percent, and eventually repealed
altogether as unworkable, was effected by the commission with rate hikes of 25 to 40 percent, in some instances higher than the railroads had dared to request.
But for the railroads, the rate bonanzas—the culmination of Colonel Fink's dream—were too good to be true.
Trucking boomed as never before—also aided by development of the pneumatic tire and the beginnings of a
national highway system—with truck registrations nearly doubling between 1920 and 1924. Rail-truck competition was on in earnest, with the trucks taking full
advantage of the ICC's railroad freight rate umbrella
and biting off ever larger chunks of railroad business,
especially the lucrative less-than-carload business. The
ICC—and the railroads—saw the light within a couple
of years and rail rates were cut back 10 percent.

The Transportation Act of 1920 had other schemes
in its power package for the ICC, and in the fulfillment
of Colonel Fink's dream. The colonel had asked that
barriers be erected against the easy entry of new rail
carriers. His memory was served on this score when the
act declared that no new line could be constructed unless the ICC had first issued a "certificate of public
convenience and necessity." The ICC was also given the
power to approve or disapprove mergers and abandon-
ments. In short, railroads were controlled coming and
going.

The regulatory net over transportation tightened during the 1930s, first with the truckers and then with the
airlines. The unregulated and highly competive truck-

ers were a sore point to the regulated railroads, as may be gauged by the following statement of the Security Owners Association, a railroad investors' group, before the National Transportation Committee headed by former President Coolidge on November 29, 1932:

> It is here suggested that the only practicable way in which highway and all other carriers operating in interstate commerce can be adequately controlled is by bringing them under the same regulations as are provided by law for railroads. In no other way can the evils which have evidenced themselves since the advent of these carriers into the transportation field be corrected, and in no other way can such carriers be made to fit into and become a valuable part of the national transportation machine.

So the truckers were brought into the cartelization picture, and the director of the ICC's fledgling Bureau of Motor Carriers became a peripatetic lecturer to the far-flung trucking industry on the fundamentals of cartelization, getting off, for example, the following velvet-gloved threats to Hartford, Connecticut, truckmen:[1]

> The Commission wants to work with the industry and wants to work with you operators . . . but we can't work with the industry if there are 57 varieties of rates in the industry. The result of that is going to be that if you folks don't get

---

[1] *Transport Topics,* December 2, 1935, quoted in Arne C. Wiprud, *Justice in Transportation,* Ziff-Davis, 1945, p. 97.

together yourselves in the interest of uniformity of rates, you may get by with it initially but a little later the Commission is going to have to prescribe them for you.

Understandably, truckmen got wise, and most cooperatively fostered truck-rate bureaus and rate conferences. Rate uniformity was the desideratum. As the commission notes of one trucking region in 1938:[1]

The evidence . . . reveals that the motor-carrier industry in this territory is in a demoralized condition due primarily to conflicting rates and practices, the lack of unity of action among respondents, and continuing rate wars.

Soon, however, when a motor conference agreed on a schedule of rates but could not force full adherence to it, it called upon the ICC to deal with the price-cutters. Mainly the ICC did this by putting the force of law— "decertification" or delicensing of any price-cutters— behind the conference-agreed-upon rates.

Rate integration was the thing but not intertransport integration. Perhaps the landmark case here is the *Pennsylvania Truck Lines*[2] case in which a Pennsylvania Railroad subsidiary sought control of Barker Motor Freight Lines to provide integrated truck-train service throughout much of Ohio. Ohio truckers protested,

---

[1]*Central Territory Motor Carrier Rates,* 8 M.C.C. 233, 253 (1938).
[2]*Pennsylvania Truck Lines-Acquisition Barker Motor Freight,* 1 M.C.C. 101; 5 M.C.C. 9; 5 M.C.C. 49.

claiming that the railroad was aiming to monopolize the trucking industry in the area and would naturally favor the railroad at the expense of its truck line, with a resulting diminution of the public interest.

The commission responded with a hedge: Trucking service could be a useful adjunct to the railroads and their customers; transportation could be coordinated and costs reduced, especially with less-than-carload shipments. But free and complete entry into trucking by railroads could be ruinous to "intermodal competition" and the healthy development of the trucking industry, or so speculated the ICC in this case. Thus, the Pennsylvania Railroad's application to create a trucking subsidiary was approved—with restrictions to make sure its trucking service was only ancillary and complementary. Similarly rail-air integration has been ruled out by the Washington way. Hence, under what has come to be known as the Barker Doctrine, the ICC has continued to restrict what may well have been fruitful integrated transport services, more effective competition, and better service to the consumer. The Canadian Pacific Railroad, to illustrate, is a strong fully integrated transport system, complete with an airline, ship lines, and truck lines, all to the benefit of the Canadian consumer.

The American consumer, on the other hand, is not so well served. For example, the ICC rejected the application of Southern Railway to reduce rates sharply on multiple-car grain shipments. Southern Railway asked for a 60 percent cut in grain haulage rates on the basis of economies resulting from use of its "Big John" hopper cars—each car designed to carry ninety tons of grain. Barge lines and truckers objected vigorously to Southern's proposal. Accordingly the ICC ordered Southern to cancel its 60 percent reduction but hinted to the railroad that it would approve a cut of 53.5 percent if Southern so reapplied. In effect, then, ICC asked Southern to keep up its rates and consumers to forego the full economic benefits of the company's five hundred special Big John hopper cars, a $13 million investment. A spokesman for the railroad, on appealing the commission's order, noted that it was a bit incongruous to "charge people $1.16 for a job we are now doing profitably for $1."[1]

For its part, the ICC, mindful to preserve competitors and not competition, defended its order in an eight to three decision as follows:[2]

> We ordered the rates to be canceled without prejudice to the filing of new schedules reflecting at least an increase of approximately 16 per cent in the multiple-car rates presently in effect. This increase would preserve the barge lines' cost advantage on certain port-to-port movements. And it would prevent the rail movement of grain at rates which would not be adequately compensatory if established on nondiscriminatory bases from Tennessee River ports.

---

[1]*Wall Street Journal,* July 23, 1963.
[2]*77th Annual Report of the Interstate Commerce Commission,* U.S. Printing Office, 1964, pp. 69-70.

Again, the ICC has long denied regional competition by maintaining port differentials on the Eastern Seaboard favoring Philadelphia, Baltimore, and Hampton Roads—the "southern tier" ports—over New York, Albany, Boston, and Portland, Maine—the "northern tier" ports. The theory of "equalization," as applied here, is to foster the sharing of import and export traffic destined for and from the inland United States. Thus, for example, export rates on six freight classifications have been three cents per hundred pounds lower to Baltimore and two cents lower to Philadelphia than to New York and Boston, and import rate differentials have been even wider—yet another case of official price discrimination against certain railroads and regions.

The equalization effort, however, was much weakened by a district court decision, affirmed by the Supreme Court, in the *Boston and Maine Railroad* case.[1] In this case, the district court vacated an ICC order directing cancellation of reduced rates proposed by railroads serving the ports of Portland, Boston, Albany, and New York. The decision was the culmination of a forty-year political struggle. The district court argued that the ICC differential failed to consider the interests of shippers, receivers, carriers, and inland communities in the northern tier. The argument recalls the ancient but telling dissenting opinion of Commissioner Clements, objecting to the ICC order of April 27, 1905,

---

[1]202 F. Supp. 830 (D. Mass. 1962) and 373 U.S. 372 (1963).

establishing differential rates in favor of Baltimore and Philadelphia:

> May competing carriers lawfully effect through the agency of the Commission restraints of competition and trade by a division of traffic between themselves and the ports when to do the same thing through an agency of their own would be unlawful? I think not. The expectation of putting these questions to ultimate rest could spring only from a Utopian dream. Their permanent rest is perhaps neither practicable in view of the interests of the ports and carriers nor desirable in the interest of the public.

The foregoing cases are illustrative actions of a determined ICC seeking to give the image of zealously protecting the public interest against collusion among various modes of transport, especially against a potentially rapacious railway system, a system allegedly monopolistic which, if it ever was, is certainly no longer monopolistic today. The market, though subverted and impeded, still has the final word. The 1968 *Annual Report* of the ICC notes that in the ten years since 1958:

> The number of regular intercity trains has declined more than 60 per cent from the 1,448 trains operated in 1958.

> Noncommutation passengers have decreased 40 per cent, and first-class passengers have dropped nearly 70 per cent.

Rail investment in new equipment for intercity service has nearly ground to a halt, and the quality of service has deteriorated in a number of instances.

Railroads have appealed to a long reluctant but recently more sympathetic ICC for permission to eliminate some of the nation's top trains, including the Chief between Chicago and Los Angeles, the Santa Fe Chief between Chicago and San Francisco, the Western Pacific's portion of the California Zephyr between San Francisco and Salt Lake City, and the Southern Pacific's Sunset between New Orleans and Los Angeles. In 1969 the Association of American Railroads voted to seek federal tax subsidies for unprofitable intercity passenger trains. In announcing the vote, Thomas M. Goodfellow, association president, said:

We still believe as firmly as ever in the free enterprise system. But we also believe that the public should support public services required of a private industry, just as they support services provided by the Post Office, and the police and fire department.

In 1970, the railroads got much of what they asked for when President Nixon signed a bill creating the National Railroad Passenger Corporation. This new semi-public corporation, known as Amtrak, is under the jurisdiction of the U.S. Department of Transportation and constitutes a rescue move to relieve the railroads of their money-losing passenger routes. It took over operation of 360 intercity passenger trains on May 1, 1971, and planned to run about half that number. Other runs will be discontinued, and, according to a Transportation Department official, the eliminations "will make what the ICC has been doing in approving discontinuances look like a picnic."[1]

Still the nation's railway system is in a sorry state of affairs. ICC regulation, state "full crew" laws, archaic union work rules—such as calling 150 train-miles a working day—have long reduced the railroads' ability to compete. In 1900 about nine out of every ten intercity freight ton-miles were by rail; in 1950 about six out of ten were by rail; and in 1970 only about four out of every ten were by rail. Today the nation's largest railroad, the $6 billion Penn Central, is in bankruptcy proceedings.

Nonetheless, the railroads are trying hard, notwithstanding the ICC, to win back their former preeminence in transportation. While long-distance passenger trains are probably a thing of the past, the railroads have moved forward with piggybacking, containerization, unit freight trains, and high-speed shuttle passenger trains such as the Penn Central's new Metroliners between New York and Washington. In addition, the railroads are perfecting data systems including TRAIN (Tele Rail Automated Information Network)—a nationwide computerized freight car-tracking system designed to deal with car distribution and localized car

---

[1]*Wall Street Journal,* November 3, 1970.

shortages; **ACI** (Automatic Car Identification)—a system for the automatic trackside identification of freight cars, which is expected to increase car utilization by as much as 10 percent; and **UMLER** (Universal Machine Language Equipment Register)—which will carry on tape a full description of all types and classes of cars, making possible the use of computers to help distribute empty freight cars to meet customer needs.

Will the railroads survive? Certainly they deserve the chance, but that chance depends on a free and open market.

And certainly something is fundamentally wrong with the ICC. The ICC has been inevitably dogged by the problem of proper economic calculation and resource allocation in the absence of true market signals and responses. Nonetheless, it has persisted in its own transportation structuring, scheduling, routing, pricing, paperwork, etc.—all such requirements being by and large unresponsive to the dynamics of the marketplace. Again, the ICC regulates not only railroads but common carrier trucks, long distance busses, moving vans, some barge lines, and oil shipment by pipeline. But even this transportation regulation is disjointed, for the CAB has the commercial airlines, the Bureau of Public Roads has the highway system, the Army Corps of Engineers has inland waterways and the Federal Maritime Commission has ocean shipping.

From the viewpoint of the railroads, all of the latter modes of transportation are heavily subsidized. Airline subsidies will be discussed in the next chapter. The

Bureau of Public Roads, financed annually from gasoline and other taxes, has subsidized the highway system —and hence indirectly trucks and busses—to the tune of $5 billion a year. The Army Corps of Engineers administers the annual rivers and harbors appropriation, a congressional pork barrel of mammoth proportions; and barges pay no tolls. Too, Federal Maritime Commission subsidies are substantial. Meanwhile, the sickness of the railroads continues.

Clearly, "consumer-protection" regulation is involved. It has forced higher costs on the shipper, carrier, and, most important of all, the consumer. The ICC should be phased out, the market should be the regulator.

CHAPTER VII

Airlines
and the Civil
Aeronautics Board

Laissez faire in public transportation cannot be expected to work. It is a dog-eat-dog way of life which, while exhilarating to the winners, cannot be counted on to serve a public interest or requirement . . .

We believe in the concept of competition. But we do not permit the rational forces of competition to resolve the type of transport available to us.

—CAB Chairman Alan S. Boyd
CAB Press Release, June 28, 1962

Chairman Boyd's hosanna to regulation can be viewed in the background of the technologically dynamic but financially ailing airline industry. As one bit of evidence of aeronautical technology, a modern Boeing 747 plane in one year can yield more available seat miles with high average daily utilization than the entire domestic trunkline industry yielded in 1945. But in recession-impacted 1970, the eleven domestic trunklines incurred a collective loss of some $200 million, compared to a profit of $370 million in 1966. Yet in the four-year period ending in 1973, U.S. airlines planned capital expenditures of some $10 billion. Most of this money was earmarked for the new "wide-bodied jets"—the Boeing 747, the McDonnell Douglas DC 10 and the Lockheed L-1011. Raising this money in the face of financial stringency will be no small matter. So perhaps regulation—the Civil Aeronautics Board—leaves something to be desired from the viewpoint of the airline industry and, more importantly, the consumer.

By law the Civil Aeronautics Board is the presumably neutral overseer of the airline industry. But the difficulty of maintaining regulatory neutrality, upholding objectivity and avoiding favoritism, apart from attaining a healthy industry, can be inferred from the swan song statement of resignation by CAB board member Louis J. Hector to President Eisenhower in 1959:[1]

> The whole system of adjudication by commissioners as practiced today inevitably raises suspicions of *ex parte* influence. Commissioners circulate more or less freely in the industry they regulate. As a part of this, there develops the social intercourse which is normal in business, executive or legislative life. When some of the

---

[1]*Yale Law Journal*, May 1960, p. 959.

groups in the industry then enter into a litigated case, the same commissioner climbs on the bench and is supposed suddenly to become a judge.

Yet the whole idea of the theoretically independent regulatory agency is, surely, independence—careful judgments unconstrained by considerations of party favor or lobby pressure, judgments neatly in line with, to quote from the controlling Civil Aeronautics Act of 1938, "the public interest, convenience and necessity"—a stock phrase for agency actions in the Fourth Branch.

Public interest, convenience, and necessity, however, are elusive concepts. The airlines regulator must somehow pick and choose among different policies, among various passenger and freight rates, among contesting airline companies, with each company bidding, with elaborate presentations complete with lawyers, witnesses, brochures, charts, statistics, etc., for the regulator's favor, especially on the critical matter of air route awards. Such awards, which can be worth millions of dollars to successful contestants, are necessarily arbitrary, bureaucratic, without a true market test. As then Chairman Boyd of the CAB conceded in the speech referred to in the heading of this chapter:

> Transportation regulation is a constant war be-
> the haves and have-nots with each of them try-
> ing to convince members of the consuming
> public that its proposals will lead to the best of
> all possible transportation worlds. Great excite-
> ment ensues with each major decision from a

regulatory agency. Each applicant has become convinced that its proposal alone comes within the scope of those magic phrases ["public interest, convenience and necessity"]. And when a proposal is not adopted, the air is rent with impassioned outcries.

Congress tried to achieve regulatory neutrality for the CAB not only by freeing it from the hegemony of any Executive department but also by having each of the five members of the board appointed by the President for six-year terms—half again as long as the presidential term, with the usual advice and consent of the Senate, and with no more than three members appointed from the same political party.

Criteria laid out for the board by Congress in the Federal Aviation Act of 1958 are as follows:

(a) The encouragement and development of an air-transportation system properly adapted to the present and future needs of the foreign and domestic commerce of the United States, of the Postal Service, and of the national defense;

(b) The regulation of air transportation in such a manner as to recognize and preserve the inherent advantages of, assure the highest degree of safety in, and foster sound economic conditions in, such transportation, and to improve the relations between, and coordinate transportation by, air carriers;

(c) The promotion of adequate, economical, and efficient service by air carriers at reasonable charges, without unjust discriminations, undue preferences or advantages, or unfair or destructive competitive practices;

(d) Competition to the extent necessary to assure the sound development of an air-transportation system properly adapted to the needs of the foreign and domestic commerce of the United States, of the Postal Services, and of the national defense;

(e) The promotion of safety in air commerce; and

(f) The promotion, encouragement, and development of Civil Aeronautics.

Obviously this is a mixed bag of goals. For example, the call for board consideration of the needs of both the Post Office and national defense, each ripe with overtones of subsidy, tends to blur the overall mission of the CAB, especially in light of its goal of fostering "sound economic conditions" and "efficient service" for air transport. And, par for the Washington way, precise criteria of soundness are nowhere to be found in the statute. The military, after all, would naturally desire a large modern commercial air fleet, competently staffed, ready in an emergency to transport war materiel and large numbers of troops to trouble spots around the world, and accordingly the larger the commercial air fleet the better. Similarly, it is quite conceivable, with the Post Office running at a loss anyway, that airmail haulage charges could be sweetened to the enhancement of the airlines—another factor hardly conducive to the development of "sound economic conditions"—or of doing right for the consumer.

Or consider another statutory goal: the board is instructed to utilize competition but only "to the extent necessary to assure the sound development" of commercial aviation. But sound development of any industry—balanced growth of the supply and demand factors—can only come over the long pull from free and open competition in the marketplace; and plainly Congress has to a large extent supplanted the market mechanism of resource allocation in the airline industry with the broad economic powers of the five-man CAB. So competition in the regulatory view is all right in the right place at the right time under the right circumstances, but again only "to the extent necessary." And the extent necessary all too frequently varies with the proclivities at the moment of the regulators. In 1943, for example, in the *TWA-North-South California Service* case, the board was apparently in a fairly procompetition frame of mind:[1]

> Since competition in itself presents an incentive to improved service and technological development, there would be a strong, although not

---

[1] 4 CAB 373 (1943).

conclusive, presumption in favor of competition on any route which offered sufficient traffic to support competing services without unreasonable increase of total operating cost.

In 1944, though in another case, the CAB apparently was in an anticompetition frame of mind:[1]

The mere fact that a particular route develops a large volume of traffic does not of itself afford sufficient justification for a finding that the public convenience and necessity require establishment of an additional competitive service exactly duplicating an existing operation.

This flip-flop, however hedged, points up the problem of different philosophies being applied by different agency administrators—or the same administrators—under differing conditions and differing pressures. Continuity and consistency of regulatory policy are thus anything but likely.

Lack of continuity and consistency of air regulation has been a continuing problem ever since the pioneers of commercial aviation pleaded that their industry be taken seriously—i.e., regulated and subsidized by a full-blown federal agency just like any other transportation industry. This plea could probably be traced all the way

---

[1] 6 CAB 217 (1944).

back to the time when the Wright brothers launched the first heavier-than-air flight on a bleak December day in 1903 over the windswept sand dunes of Kitty Hawk on the North Carolina coast. The U.S. Army— one source of subsidy—took some interest in the military potential of the new invention, but between 1903 and the U.S. declaration of war in 1917 only two hundred planes, military and nonmilitary, were produced, each one practically obsolete by the time of its maiden flight.

With American entry in World War I came the war-born panic of the military to create an air force almost overnight: In the initial twelve wartime months procurement orders totaled thirty thousand planes. Yet the hurried production program was hardly able to put a single U.S.-built plane into combat. After the Armistice, war-surplus planes were dumped on the market for about 1 percent or less of their original cost, and the vast aircraft production facilities were put on the block. Regular aircraft production was virtually out of commission for nearly a decade. This feast-and-famine cycle for the aircraft industry was repeated with World War II, the Korean War, and the Vietnam War.

In any event, airmail became the main vehicle for subsidy—and regulation. In 1918, fifteen years after the Kitty Hawk flight, the Post Office Department won a $100 thousand appropriation for experimental airmail runs between New York and Washington. The Army detailed three Curtiss JN-4 training aircraft for the job. President Wilson launched the inaugural flight from Washington, but the pilot got lost in Maryland, made

an emergency landing, and the mail had to be ignomi-
nously brought back to Washington by car.

Still, such a setback was not enough to long deter the
airborne couriers from the swift completion of their
appointed rounds. Airmail flying finally became com-
monplace, even if flying the mail at the outset was most
hazardous. Of the forty mail pilots, including a young
barnstormer by the name of Charles A. Lindbergh,
hired by the Post Office, thirty-one lost their lives in the
line of duty. This fact, plus the Billy Mitchell court
martial and a number of military aircraft crashes, led
to President Coolidge's apointment of Dwight Morrow
to conduct a public investigation of U.S. aviation. One
recommendation made by Morrow was to transfer the
airmail operation from the Post Office to private contractors.

Initial recipients of airmail contracts were fledgling
airlines, mostly combination mail-passenger carriers.
Civil Air Mail Route No. 1, for example, went to
Colonial Airlines (now merged into Eastern Airlines)
which flew mail between Boston and New York. The
fledglings grew, especially with the 1927 flight of the
Lone Eagle from New York to Paris in little more than
thirty-three hours, a feat which greatly helped to increase air passenger travel and thereby served to dimin-
ish, to a degree, the financial dependence of air carriers
on airmail contracts. Technology also aided the young
airlines with superior aircraft like the Ford Trimotor
and the Boeing "Flying Pullman" Trimotor. In 1929
United flew sixty-one hundred passengers into Chicago,

a considerable number in those days. Commercial aviation was catching on.

The Morrow recommendation to the Coolidge Administration for development of commercial aviation through airmail awards to commercial airlines extended to the succeeding Hoover Administration. Hoover's postmaster general, Walter Folger Brown, a budding interventionist, took most seriously his express portfolio assignment "to encourage commercial aviation . . . and contract for the airmail service." Postmaster General Brown was unhappy over the fact that, with the exception of United Airlines, the airline business was made up of some forty marginal firms. Practically all of them were, by his lights, underfinanced, undersized, underequipped, all quite dependent on airmail contracts—the distribution of which on a competitive bid basis reminded the postmaster general of a "kennel at feeding time,"[1] with each carrier struggling against the others for a meaty chunk of public funds. So, in his view, consolidation was in order.

Brown had the formidable leverage of airmail contracts to bring about his consolidation plan, and he used it to forge two new major airlines and two additional transcontinental routes in addition to United's—TWA, one merger product, getting the central route and American, the other outgrowth of consolidation, the southern route.

---

[1]Quoted in Charles J. Kelly, Jr., *The Sky's the Limit,* Coward-Mc-Cann, 1963, p. 72.

With the victory of the New Deal in 1932, this Republican allocation did not sit well with Democrat Senator Hugo Black who headed a special Senate committee investigating the awarding of airmail contracts. Both Senator Black and the Democratic majority of his committee were especially curious about the alliances between Brown and the big airline operators. Senator Black, now a Supreme Court justice, was armed with material collected by Fulton Lewis, Jr., then a young Hearst reporter. Both Lewis and Black picked up information from dissident small carriers excluded from the Brown "negotiations."

Among the Black committee's charges: lower bids by smaller carriers had frequently been rejected in favor of higher bids by the larger operators. Concluded Senator Black, commenting on what he labeled the Post Office's "spoils conferences":[1]

> The control of American aviation has been ruthlessly taken away from the men who could fly and bestowed upon bankers, brokers, promoters, and politicians sitting in their inner offices, allotting among themselves the taxpayers' money.

Senator Black convinced FDR that the airmail contracts were crooked, and in February 1934 the President huffily handed the job of flying the mail to the Army

---

[1] *Ibid.,* p. 91.

Air Corps. The action, to put it mildly, was capricious. The army pilots had neither specialized planes nor experience. Within a week a stunned nation witnessed dozens of crashes costing the lives of twelve army pilots and seriously injuring others. In theory the army was called in to arrest "exhorbitant" airline profits, but the average cost of flying the mail under the army came to more than four times the amount under the airlines. Lindbergh entered the fray, sending the following telegram to President Roosevelt:

> Your present action does not discriminate between innocence and guilt and places no premium on honest business. Your order of cancellation of all air mail contracts condemns the largest portion of our commercial aviation without just trial.

The Air Mail Act of 1934 reopened all airmail routes to competitive bidding, ordered aircraft production divorced from the airlines and lodged regulatory control in no less than three different agencies: the Bureau of Air Commerce to regulate technical and safety aspects; the Post Office to award airmail contracts on the basis of competitive bids and to establish routes and schedules; and the Interstate Commerce Commission to fix mail pay for each route to preclude unreasonable profits —or losses.

The wonders of Washington: the loss-absorption feature was obviously at odds with the competitive-bid feature. This situation gave rise in 1938 to Braniff's bargain-basement, mail-route contract bid of $0.0000-

1907378 per airplane mile between Houston and San Antonio, a bid nonetheless higher than Eastern's bid of zero cents per mile, each airline fully expecting that an understanding ICC would bail them out of their inevitable red-ink condition should they win the contract. Even so, the airlines considered the 1934 law sadly deficient in several important respects: It still called for too much competition and too many regulatory agencies, and was apparently still too powerless to prevent losses which were mounting fast during the Great Depression. The head of the newly-formed Air Transport Association spoke out, pleading for government assistance:[1]

> Of the $120,000,000 of private investment which has been made in American air transport, more than half is gone. This condition of financial starvation not only makes it impossible for these lines to take full advantage of possible technological improvements, but could lead to traffic competition of such intensity that the accident ratio might accelerate instead of decline. Failure to correct the existing situation and to do so promptly, means more than loss to the capital remaining invested in the air transport industry, to the labor employed in it, and to this country's position in civil aviation. It may very well entail a large cost in human life.

The upshot of such pressure was the Civil Aeronautics Act of 1938, an act which gave the airlines pretty

---

[1]Kelly, *op. cit.*, p. 101.

much all they wanted, including the creation of their own regulatory agency (the Civil Aeronautics Board), the protection of airline routes through the so-called "grandfather" clause, and the awarding of mail pay on the basis of need and no longer by competitive bid. After all, the railroads, trucks, busses, shipping lines, and pipelines had the government's helping and protecting hand; why should commercial aviation be treated as an outsider? So Congress froze the basic route structure, thereby reducing competition to a minimum, and stood ready—in the absence of course of fraud and gross inefficiency by management—not only to make up any loss on operations but to guarantee some return on investment. Thus for a loss-ridden, government-harassed industry, the act was a happy victory, practically a blank check.

If there was a rub to the act, it seemed like a trifle— the empowering of the Civil Aeronautics Board as virtual economic czar over commercial aviation. The board, then and now, has much to say: The board must "certificate" all air routes and carriers—no certificate means no route and no route means in effect no carrier, no airline; the board decides which airline shall serve which cities and how often; it passes on all passenger, freight, and mail rates set by the carriers; and when, upon complaint or upon its own initiative, it finds these charges to be other than "just and reasonable" it can fix maximum or minimum rates or both; the board also sees that air service is rendered free from "unjust discriminations" and "undue preference and advantage"; it subsidizes needy airlines and approves mergers and route consolidations; and it requires airlines to submit periodically their accounts, records, contracts, and reports.

This, then, is the CAB package. The in-group of trunklines was now really in—the CAB made the airline cartel club a most exclusive one. In its entire career, a time of tremendous expansion of commercial aviation, the board has not aproved a single new trunkline application.

Yet, while impeding entry into the industry by outsiders—among them possibly creative innovators—the grandfather clause has been no guarantee of success in the cartel club. This can be seen in the attrition in the grandfather ranks from the nineteen domestic trunkline carriers originally certificated in 1938 to eleven in 1970: American, Braniff, Continental, Delta, Eastern, National, Northeast, Northwest, TWA, United and Western. Most of the attrition was a matter of weak or failing companies being merged or absorbed into the stronger airlines with, of course, the necessary blessing of the CAB. The CAB approved, for example, United's acquisition of Capitol Airlines in 1961 but later quashed the marriage plans of Eastern and American and of TWA and Pan American.

The CAB's authority extends from the trunklines to the supplemental or charter carriers, the suburban or air taxi carriers and the local service or "feeder" carriers, including Alaskan and Hawaiian carriers. The feeders are the result of a CAB experiment shortly after the end of World War II to furnish air service on a regional basis to smaller communities and thus to link them with major terminals. To be sure, this laudable idea is not exactly the brainchild of the board. With war-surplus DC-3s being dumped on the market for $20 thousand or less, it seemed that every ex-air corps pilot and his brother wanted to cash in on the airline boom —and to secure the support of his local Congressman to do it. Naturally, like all infant industries, a subsidy would be required, "temporarily" of course, just long enough to see that the feeders reached young adulthood. (But infancy almost always seems so much longer when a subsidy is around.)

The thought of more competition, and subsidized competition at that, struck horror into the supposedly sinecured grandfather carriers. If there was to be air service to the hinterland, they would gladly provide it— with the taxpayers chipping in to make up any deficit. The grandfathers, though, lost out to the grass-roots movement, as can be seen in the CAB rationale in the *Rocky Mountain States Air Service* case:[1]

> In view of the limited traffic potentialities of the points on the new system, an unusual effort will be required to develop the maximum traffic. Greater effort and the exercise of managerial ingenuity may be expected from an independent local operator whose continuation in the air transportation business will depend upon the successful development of traffic on the routes and the operation of the service on an adequate and economical basis.

[1] 6 CAB 695 (1946).

Accordingly the CAB launched—in CAB parlance, certificated—some twenty such feeders as Bonanza, Central, Ozark, Pacific, Piedmont, Trans-Texas, and West Coast. By the end of the sixties there were but nine surviving lines. At first "temporary" certificates were issued to the feeders. This condition only exacerbated their financing and recruiting problems as investors and personnel understandably did not take wholeheartedly to carriers whose terms of existence were ever in doubt. However, in 1955 Congress showed mercy on the "experimental" feeders and ordered the CAB to grant them permanent certificates.

But adding to the dilemma of the feeders was the announced policy of the Board that they were not to challenge the trunks competitively— not, in other words, to let competition get out of hand. Congressmen have been generally most friendly to the local service carriers, especially as air transportation has become a staple commodity in the business world and local politicians generally have to answer their constituents on any lack of air service. In 1960, for example, a bill introduced by Senator Jennings Randolph (D., W. Va.) and supported by the Senate Commerce Committee would have forced the board in route-case procedures to require trunk carriers to hand over underused routes to the feeders.

Although the bill did not get very far, its suggestion did not fall on deaf ears, and feeders have been accumulating the thin routes of the trunks for some time. For example, in 1964 the CAB approved the transfer of TWA's operating rights to local service carriers for certain short-haul routes to and from Williamsport and Scranton, Pennsylvania, and Binghamton and Albany, New York, cities now served by Allegheny and Mohawk Airlines.

But the feeders were not always so lucky nor were their Congressional friends always able to make their influence felt. Consider, for instance, the anticompetition stance—a stance obviated by later feeder development and CAB flip-flop policy—in the *Bonanza-TWA Route Transfer* case:[1]

> We would like to emphasize again that we have neither the disposition nor the intention to permit local air carriers to metamorphose into trunk lines competitive with the permanently certificated trunk lines. The local service carriers were certificated by us as an experimental effort to bring useful air transportation services into the smaller communities and the isolated or sparsely populated areas of this country and to feed connecting traffic to long-haul carriers. We recognize that some competition between local service carriers and trunk lines is inevitable but we intend not only to minimize such competition but to prevent its development to the greatest feasible extent.

The forces that gave rise to the feeders—plenty of ex-air corps pilots and cheap war-surplus DC-3s—also gave rise to the supplemental air carriers, more com-

---

[1] 10 CAB 893 (1949).

monly known as the nonskeds. The theory of the non-skeds seems to have been a sound one. Rather than operate on fixed schedules and routes, the nonskeds could achieve capacity or near-capacity operations by making fast adjustments in air traffic movements. In this way they could cut unit costs and hence passenger fares and cargo rates. Naturally, at the outset a lot of business gravitated to the nonskeds. This brought out-cries from the scheduled airlines that the nonsked coach flights were economically unsound and a danger to the future of commercial aviation. At first the CAB ignored the outcries, inadvertently prodding the scheduled air-lines into meeting the competitive thrust and starting up their own economy coach service which continues to the present day. The scheduled airlines, however, still kept up pleas for relief from the nonskeds.

Initially the nonskeds were exempted from regulation under the 1938 law, but in 1947 the CAB, harkening to pleas from the scheduled airlines, brought the non-skeds into the regulatory fold by requiring them to regi-ster with the board. The "problem" for the regulators was that the irregular coach operators were running practically a regular route service on long-haul runs, and this was competition with the trunks that the regu-lators felt had to stop. It did, mainly due to such CAB harassment as a strict numerical limit of ten scheduled flights per month between any pair of cities. The some one hundred fifty nonskeds in 1949 had shrunk to less than fifty a decade later and number but about a dozen today. So once again we see that regulation can mean anything but security for those who are regulated, or economy for those who are supposedly benefitted—the consumers.

Now, just how secure are the trunk lines under CAB policy? Northeast, to cite a case, in the CAB's three-to-two decision in August 1963 was refused permanent certification of the carrier's vital New York-Florida route. Northeast and some formidable allies fought the decision. Allies Edward Kennedy and Leverett Salton-stall, respectively Democratic and Republican Senators from Massachusetts, asked the Justice Department in 1964 to investigate antitrust ramifications of the decision which, by eliminating Northeast, left only two carriers—Eastern and National—on the lucrative New York-Florida run.

The Justice Department, then under the direction of Attorney General Robert Kennedy, responded by attacking the CAB's decision, claiming Northeast's withdrawal yielded a "monopolistic value" to Eastern and National, and requested permission to "intervene" in the case. The board summarily rejected the intervention plea, reminding the department that hearings on the case had been going on for two years during which time nothing had been heard from the Justice Department. Meanwhile, Northeast by one legal strategem or another managed to keep flying to Florida—long past the deadline of November 15, 1963, set by the CAB. Pressure and persistence got results; permanent CAB certification was won by Northeast in March 1967.

But pressure is an old story to the CAB and to every other regulatory agency ever beseiged by attorneys, witnesses, politicians, lobbyists, industry people, and other interested parties—but rarely, if ever, by the consumer. For example, in the Northeast case not the consumer but the following parties filed petitions or briefs during one phase of the hearings:

> Air Line Pilots Association,
> International Association of Machinists,
> Master Executive Council of the Pilots of
>   Northeast Airlines,
> The State of New Hampshire,
> The Commonwealth of Massachusetts,
> The Massachusetts Port Authority,
> The New England Council,
> The Mayor and City Council of Baltimore, Md.,
> The Baltimore Association of Commerce,
> The Cities and/or Chambers of Commerce of
>   Bangor, Me., Boston, Mass., Manchester, N.H.,
>   Philadelphia, Pa., and Portland, Me.
> Eastern Air Lines,
> National Airlines,
> The States of Maine and Vermont,
> The Department of Justice.

Sometimes the regulators strike back at the pressure-pushers. In 1963, to cite one instance, the CAB released material charging that the Air Transport Association, which is made up of all the nation's scheduled airlines, engaged in "activities designed to bring pressure on the board to obtain favorable decisions based on pressure rather than on the merit of the cases."[1] Among the

---

[1] *Wall Street Journal*, August 2, 1963.

documents which had been subpoenaed by the board
and released to the public were letters and memoranda
from the ATA's private files. One memorandum from
an ATA vice-president to the association's president,
dated 1957, was concerned with a program aimed "to
thoroughly indoctrinate the Civil Aeronautics Board
and staff" and suggested "an organized campaign to
find out who has influence on the individual members
and a followup to educate those people."

Still, bureaucratic sensitivity to pressure seems endemic to regulation. Even so small a thing as a telephone
call from a politician can send tremors throughout the
CAB, as Charles J. Kelly, Jr., a former CAB lawyer,
noted:[1]

> When I was at the CAB, I used to be amazed
> at the crisis of handwringing created by any
> telephone call from a Senator. In most cases,
> the Senator in question had no strong personal
> convictions in the case. The calls generally were
> made to impress a constituent, important either
> because of employment in the Senator's state
> or for campaign contributions. Actually, to my
> observation, such calls were generally self-
> canceling as far as benefiting any one airline,
> since every company has a Senator from its
> home state. The real damage from Congres-
> sional pressures seemed to me to be a tendency
> on the part of the Board to try to give a little

---

[1]Kelly, *op. cit.*, pp. 295–296.

something to everybody, rather than seek the best decision regardless.

Rate pressure is particularly pronounced. Some years ago CAB Chairman Boyd criticized the growing multiplicity of experimental fare plans—one-class service, two-class service, three-class service, husband-and-wife plans, family plans, shuttle service, economy service, military fares, student fares, "Visit-U.S.A." fares, etc.— as a "can of worms"—although most of these plans continue today with CAB blessing. Mr. Boyd also stated that he, too, favored experimentation, but felt that there had to be an "orderly flow," that he would like to keep the fare "chaos under control." As it is, what considerable rate uniformity remains does produce its own competitive anomalies—movies, pillows, slippers, use of typewriters and electric shavers, champagne, and other epicurean delights varying from one airline to another, each airline boasting that it has the most beautiful, charming, designer-clad hostesses, and the like, all of which are not so "chaotic" (Mr. Boyd's word) as they are in fact competitive.

All this fare experimentation and service innovation —aspects of quality competition as they are—are of course of interest to the student of competition, and at first-blush they bespeak vigorous competition; but it is clear that there are competitive walls that no carrier is permitted to scale, and there are floors under rates, below which no carrier is permitted to price.

The consumer, however, gets a competitive break in California where the CAB's rate-making jurisdiction does not reach the strictly intrastate Pacific Southwest Airlines. This aggressive price-cutting airline, in competition with TWA, United and Western, flies about as many intrastate passengers as all other airlines in California put together, originating more than one thousand flights per week. "Little" PSA's ability to compete with the giants by sharp price-cutting, high-grade equipment, frequent flights, and an excellent safety record is one more testimonial to free competition and free enterprise. Yet this testimonial could not have been written were it not for a quirk in federal and California jurisdictional authority—the fact that the interstate CAB cannot reach intrastate PSA and that the California Public Utility Commission cannot undo fare cuts initiated by PSA and opposed by a host of wounded competitors. And maybe it could not have been written were it not for the further fact that PSA has never received tax subsidies or mail revenues.

The consumer also gets a similar competitive break in transatlantic air travel, thanks to the audacity of Icelandic Airlines opting out of the antitrust-proof, U.S. government-approved International Air Transport Association (IATA)—an international cartel agreement signed by the State Department in Chicago on December 7, 1944, and reinforced by bilateral air transport agreements with practically every major country in the world. IATA sets international air fares and, not unlike the CAB, sets them with monopoly on its mind. TWA, Pan American, Northwest, Braniff International, and other U.S. carriers making foreign stops all subscribe to IATA fares. The American air traveler wishing to beat

the cartel, however, can choose the PSA of the international airlines—Icelandic. Icelandic is the only pri-
vately-owned, nonsubsidized, noncartelized, scheduled
foreign airline in the transatlantic service, and one of
the very few in the world which has never received a
subsidy nor had a fatal crash. It flies CL-44s built by
Canadair, a subsidiary of General Dynamics, and leased
DC-8s. In 1953, when the airline started, Icelandic
carried eight hundred passengers. In 1970 it carried
some two hundred and fifty thousand. The range of
savings of Icelandic over IATA fares between New
York and London and between New York and Luxem-
bourg ranges from 10 to 30 percent, although Icelandic
is not permitted nonstop service between those points.

In 1971, however, the international airline cartel
cracked more than a bit as a wave of transatlantic
"youth fare" cuts spread from airline to airline, mostly
to the $210–220 peak season round-trip level. (See
Chapter 2 for Adam Smith's observation on how cartels tend to break down.) Alitalia led the parade with
a cut to $199 round-trip fare applying to persons 12 to
25 years old traveling between Philadelphia, Boston, or
New York and Rome or Milan. Alitalia has said its
$199 fare was ordered by the Italian government. But
the Justice Department, acting on behalf of the CAB,
asked a federal district court in New York for a temporary restraining order barring the Italian carrier
from selling tickets and carrying passengers between
the U.S. and Italy at the allegedly illegal fare. So Alitalia halted its sale of youth-fare transatlantic tickets.
The Italian carrier told a judge it would stop the sales

after the judge said he would sign a temporary injunction sought by the CAB against the cut-rate fare. Again, a regulatory agency revealed its basic anticonsumer, proproducer bias. The CAB doesn't need to take lessons from IATA on cartelizing industry, however, and it is interesting to speculate on how American commercial aviation might have fared in the absence of the CAB. For, in addition to restricting entry and price competition, the CAB has subsidized the airlines directly and the government has subsidized them indirectly through airport construction, traffic control, navigational aids, and weather information. Local service carriers, however, still received the bulk of some $55 million in direct subsidies in fiscal 1968, down about $9 million from fiscal 1967, and the CAB believes that the downward subsidy trend will continue.

The long and short of CAB regulation has been that commercial aviation has been treated as a giant subsidized public utility, managerial decision-making has been impeded, consumer sovereignty frustrated, economies of scale blunted, innovations and technological efficiency in airlines operations hampered.

The final question remains: Which should be the proper mechanism for resolving the supply and demand considerations of commercial aviation—the market or the CAB, competition or interventionism? While the benign regulation of the Federal Aviation Authority (FAA) is desirable for air safety and should of course be retained, the CAB should be phased out of existence with its air-safety functions transferred to the FAA.

CHAPTER VIII

Broadcasters, Viewers, Listeners and the Federal Communications Commission

You are not merely babysitting electronically. You are molding, by the hand and heart and mind, America's future. You chose a hard life when you chose broadcasting. You volunteered for public regulation and public pressure. In return, the people have placed in your hands the greatest gift possible in a free country, the extraordinary privilege of using the public airwaves of others, who would welcome, indeed have fought for, that privilege.

—Newton N. Minow,
Chicago, April 4, 1963

So the then chairman of the Federal Communications Commission, the crusading Mr. Minow, never one to mince words, addressed the nation's broadcasters assembled in convention in Chicago in 1963. The Minow belief that commercial TV is, by his own description, a "vast wasteland," a cultural desert of Westerns, mayhem, and mindless situation comedies and a clamorous casbah of commercials upon commercials which plead, bleat, pressure, groan, and shout, seems to be shared by members of the Federal Communications Commission preceding and succeeding Mr. Minow. The Minow crusade demonstrated strained FCC-broadcaster relations and some portent of the power over broadcasting —and the consumer—wielded by the FCC.

The FCC is an "independent" agency charged with the complex job of regulating interstate and foreign communications via radio, television, telephone, telegraph, satellite, and cable. The seven commission members are appointed by the President with the advice and consent of the Senate for seven-year terms with the stipulation that not more than four members may be of the same party. The chairman's tenure is at the pleasure of the President. After almost a half century of regulation, the commission's empire has grown to some sixty-five hundred AM and FM radio stations and one thousand television stations.

Power wielded by the commissioners also includes utility regulation of rates and services of the nation's telephone and telegraph systems, including the world's largest corporation, the American Telephone & Telegraph Company. The rate-setting power over the "common-carrier" services of telephone and telegraph companies has obvious political appeal. For example, within a year after Franklin D. Roosevelt signed the Communications Act of 1934, the FCC, acting on a Senate resolution, launched a rate-making investigation of the telephone industry. In 1936, the commission ordered a reduction in interstate and long-distance telephone rates of $19.35 million annually. Other rate cuts were ordered over the years and occasionally a rate boost. In November 1964 the FCC ordered the American Telephone & Telegraph Company to reduce interstate telephone rates by about $100 million annually. And in 1965 the commission began a massive rate-making investigation of AT&T and associated Bell System companies, a move that helped send the price of AT&T common stock into a long decline representing a multi-billion-dollar loss to AT&T shareholders.

One upshot of the investigation (sixty-six witnesses, more than ten thousand pages of testimony with 3,485 additional pages of exhibit material) came on July 5, 1967, when the commission set a return of 7 to 7½ percent on AT&T's telephone investment and ordered a reduction of $120 million annually in interstate rates. The company's 1968 annual report rebutted that technological advances and increasing efficiency were unable to overcome "the inflationary pace of rising costs," adding:

We feel strongly that under present conditions Bell System earnings should be in the range of at least 8½ per cent on total capital. Every year, to meet demands for service, $1½ billion or more must be obtained in the financial markets. We must compete for this money at a time when interest rates are the highest in half a century. Further, we must continuously compete with other businesses for the favor of equity investors—share owners—who in these inflationary times look for growth in earnings and dividends to prevent erosion of their investment.

The 8½ percent return looks modest in view of the 9 percent paid by some Bell companies on bonds issued in 1970.

Besides regulatory power over the telephone and telegraph industry, the FCC commissioners have extensive regulatory—in the main, licensing—power over broadcasting. It is this power that is the chief concern of this chapter. Under law the commissioners pass upon all license applications for radio and TV stations. Their power also includes assignment of frequencies, transmission power, operating times, and call letters; inspection of equipment; passing upon changes in station ownership or facilities; and reviewing station operations before renewing licenses. Each license runs for a three-year period and, upon reapplication, is considered for renewal. At license renewal time, the commission reviews the overall performance of a station to determine whether it has lived up to the obligations and promises made when it was licensed or relicensed to operate.

In deference to the First Amendment, the commissioners are specifically enjoined from censoring programs or interfering with the right of free speech on the air. But while the commissioners do not prescribe percentages of time for the broadcast of particular subjects they have adopted a broad policy on programming as a general guide for broadcasters. The law also says that broadcast stations are not common carriers such as telephones and telegraph; hence, the commissioners do not regulate the broadcasters' accounting methods, time charges, return on equity, etc., nor do they license networks as such—only individual stations. They prescribe that one owner cannot operate more than one station of the same kind—AM, FM, or TV—in the same community, or more than seven like stations in the country as a whole, but of the seven TV stations allowed, no more than five can be VHF outlets, with the other two being the less popular UHF outlets. The FCC is also concerned with the frequency and "loudness" of commercials but the Federal Trade Commission, as noted, has jurisdiction over false and misleading advertising over the air.

Within these regulatory boundaries, the FCC has wide latitude in exercising its licensing prerogative over American broadcasting. The overriding question, though, is, Is this regulation necessary? Particularly, is there another and better way to allocate radio frequencies and TV channels and police the airwaves than the FCC-Washington way? As Professor Louis Jaffe of the Harvard Law School noted:[1]

> Seven men in Washington are giving away broadcasting channels worth millions of dollars —apparently with no clear guide except personal whims and political pressure.

The basis for Professor Jaffe's observation of FCC

---

[1]Louis Jaffe, "The Scandal in TV Licensing," *Harper's Magazine,* September 1957.

largesse is a widely held view that the "public" (translation: the U.S. government) "owns" the nation's airwaves. This view also accounts for Mr. Minow's preachments to the broadcasters in his "wasteland" speech:[1]

> Your license lets you use the public's airwaves as trustees for 180 million Americans. The public is your beneficiary. If you want to stay on as trustees, you must deliver a decent return to the public—not only to your stockholders. . . . For every hour that the public gives you—you owe them something. I intend to see that your debt is paid with service.

So the airwaves, vast as they are, are looked upon as a gigantic government preserve, nominally in the hands of the American people who grant trusteeship through the FCC to the broadcasters.

But it wasn't always thus. When radio first came into existence around the turn of the century with its initial dot-dash signals, there was little need for legal intervention or government regulation. The broadcasting spectrum was broad and interference on the part of one station in the frequency of another was minimal. But by the end of the first decade of the twentieth century a broadcasting cacophony—the emergence of more than one station signal on the same frequency—was a growing problem. As the Department of the Navy explained in a letter to the Senate Commerce Committee dated

---

[1]*Vital Speeches,* June 15, 1961.

March 30, 1910, each radio station claimed the right "to send forth its electric waves through the ether at any time that it may desire, with the result that there exists in many places a state of chaos."

The Navy Department suggested some kind of government control over all radio stations as a solution to interference. The upshot of this and other petitioning was passage in 1912 of an act of Congress requiring that radio station operators have a license issued by the Secretary of Commerce setting forth the ownership and location of each station and its assigned frequency and hours of operation. The rub developed, however, that the Secretary had to license all comers under the 1912 act. Within a few years the air was crowded to a point that interference was again widespread. To cope with interference, a bill was introduced in Congress to give the Post Office a monopoly of all wireless communications. And in 1917 Secretary of the Navy Josephus Daniels asked that the Navy Department be given "the exclusive ownership, of all wireless communication for commercial purposes." But little was done, save that licensing became even more restrictive as to permissible hours of operation.

The restrictions were widely considered intolerable. In 1925 the Zenith Corporation was brought into court for violation of the 1912 act. Zenith had overridden Secretary of Commerce Hoover's licensing restrictions of the wavelength of 332.4 meters and hours of operation limited to 10:00 P.M. to 12:00 P.M. on Thursdays, provided that such hours were not wanted by General Electric's Denver station. Zenith was naturally not happy with the miniscule arrangement and decided to challenge the Secretary. As a result of a court decision in 1926 upholding Zenith,[1] Secretary Hoover was not only compelled to issue licenses to all applicants but the licensees were free to set their own station power, frequency, and hours of operation. Within nine months of the decision, two hundred more stations came into being, with interference at an all-time peak and the audience tuning out. Radio advertising revenues began to turn downward. Radio set sales fell off, and radio manufacturers beseeched Congress for thorough regulatory policing in order to prevent interference and "save the industry." Meanwhile, the Senate passed a resolution declaring the airwaves to be "the inalienable possession of the people of the United States:[2]

The resolution was a forerunner of the Federal Radio Act of 1927 calling for tight licensing control over the radio industry. The 1927 pattern of regulatory authority is basically the pattern of today, with the Communications Act of 1934 transferring the powers of the Federal Radio Commission to the present Federal Communications Commission so as to centralize federal regulation of wire and wireless communication. The Federal Radio Act created an independent regulatory agency, and all previous licensing loopholes were closed. Licenses were to be issued only when the "public interest, necessity, or convenience would be served"; licensees had to use only

---

[1]*U.S.* v. *Zenith Radio Corp.*, 12 F.(2d) 614 (N.D., Ill., 1926).
[2]R. H. Coase, "The Federal Communications Commission," *The Journal of Law and Economics,* October 1956, p. 5.

their assigned frequency or frequencies, use no others, and sign a waiver of any claim to permanent use of a frequency; stations could not rebroadcast, without permission, programs originated on other stations; program sponsors had to be identified.

In addition, Congress, aware of the First Amendment, specifically sought to safeguard free speech. The First Amendment to the Constitution, it will be remembered, reads as follows:

> Congress shall make no law respecting an establishment of religion or prohibiting the free exercise thereof; or abridging the freedom of speech, or of the press; or the right of the people peaceably to assemble, and to petition the Government for a redress of grievances.

Section 326 of the Communications Act of 1934, as amended, provides that:

> Nothing in this chapter shall be understood or construed to give the Commission the power of censorship over the radio communications or signals transmitted by any radio station, and no regulation or condition shall be promulgated or fixed by the Commission which shall interfere with the right of free speech by means of radio communication.

But the 1934 act goes on and qualifies the guarantee of free speech by its ban on "obscene, indecent or profane" language. In addition, stations giving air time to legally qualified political candidates have to extend equal time to all other qualified candidates. These restrictions may not unduly wrench the Constitution but, as we will see, they become slippery with regulatory interpretation. Perhaps the basic FCC conflict with the First Amendment lies in the licensing power itself. In 1943, in the revealing case of *NBC* v. *United States,* the Supreme Court described this licensing prerogative as follows:[1]

> An important element of public interest and convenience affecting the issue of a license is the ability of the licensee to render the best practicable service to the community reached by broadcasts . . . The Commission's licensing function cannot be discharged, therefore, merely by finding that there are no technological objections to the granting of a license. If the criterion of "public interest" were limited to such matters, how could the Commission choose between two applicants for the same facilities, each of whom is financially and technically qualified to operate a station?

Under this logic, the FCC says who can broadcast and, in effect, who cannot—a discriminatory power at odds with freedom of the press, a power, in short, of censorship. Just how does the FCC decide among competing applicants? One requirement is that the applicant must be an American citizen. Character of the

---

[1]319 U.S. 190 (1943).

applicant is also a factor. In 1964, for example, the license of the two owners of radio station WGMA, Hollywood, Florida, Daniel Enright and Jack Barry, both of whom figured in fixed TV quiz show scandals in the late fifties, was not renewed on grounds of lack of character qualifications.[1] Also, the applicant must show that, as a rather strict rule, he will promote local, wholesome, diversified, and independent programming. Licenses have been withdrawn on the charge that supposedly there was "no attempt to determine the program needs" of affected localities. Occasionally delicensing is accompanied by a fine. In June 1967, for example, the commission issued a forfeiture order against Eastern Broadcasting Corp., former licensee of station WALT in Tampa, Florida, and imposed the statutory maximum fine of $10 thousand on the company for conducting an allegedly fraudulent contest.

Thus, as will be further illustrated, license denials involve censorship, as much as if the *New York Times* was officially denied publication rights on grounds that it somehow had not accommodated the newspaper needs of New York. Nonetheless, the courts have upheld the authority of the FCC to interest itself in the licensee's programming. Further, the "public" has egged the commission into action. According to a recent FCC annual report, the commission received more than fifty-nine thousand expressions of public opinion, mostly letters, on broadcasting matters, of which some twenty-two thousand were complaints. Of the latter, the vast

---

[1]*Wall Street Journal,* April 20, 1964.

majority were concerned about program content and advertising practices over the air, and 7.5 percent of all complaints were about political broadcasts and editorializing.

Complaints go into the FCC's files on individual stations and can be brought out at renewal time to straighten out an errant renewal applicant. Understandably no station owner wants a lot of letters in its file at the FCC to raise the eyebrows of the commissioners. In a 1960 statement on programming policy, which the commission describes as neither "rigid" nor "all-embracing," the following fourteen items are listed as the major elements "usually necessary" to meet "the public interest, convenience and necessity" of the community in which the station is located:

Opportunity for Local Self-Expression
Development and Use of Local Talent
Programs for Children
Religious Programs
Educational Programs
Public Affairs Programs
Editorialization by Licensees
Political Broadcasts
Agricultural Programs
News Programs
Weather and Market Reports
Sports Programs
Service to Minority Groups
Entertainment Programming

Thus it becomes plain that the broadcaster's leeway

over programming is anything but complete—the more so under the FCC's license renewal criterion of performance measured against promise. Thus, for example, if a licensee were to promise six hours weekly of programs for children or four hours for religion, he cannot much reduce or drop that total time without likely having to answer to the commission at renewal itme.

While a license, once granted by the FCC, has been nearly always renewed, renewal is not automatic, less so now than in the past. A case in point is the commission's refusal in 1969 to renew the license of Boston station WHDH-TV operated for ten years by a Boston newspaper, the *Boston Herald-Traveler.* The license was awarded instead to a newly organized group known as Boston Broadcasters, Inc., one of several contenders for the prized license. Weighing against the *Herald-Traveler,* but not considered material by the FCC, was the measurement of performance as matched against original promises made to obtain the license. Considered material, however, was the promise by untested Boston Broadcasters to perform better in the future than tested *Herald-Traveler* had performed in the past. But weighing most heavily against the operators of WHDH-TV was the fact that the station was owned by a local newspaper. If the Boston decision sets a policy precedent, the FCC frown on newspaper ownership of broadcast stations could affect some 250 daily newspapers with broadcast outlets in the same city in which they publish.

If the Boston case is indeed a portent of future decisions, the FCC appears to be embarking on a tough new renewal policy favoring "integration of ownership and management" and opposing multiple broadcasting operations and joint newspaper-television or radio ownership. The nature of ownership looms large in FCC thinking, as evidenced in a 1968 proceeding when the commission proposed only-one-to-a-customer broadcast licenses be granted in a single geographical market. This would prevent a local TV station from owning an AM or FM radio station or vice versa.

That the ownership issue is hot and that broadcast licenses may be increasingly up for grabs before an FCC bent on changing ownership patterns can be seen in FCC Commissioner Nicholas Johnson's open invitation on WRC-TV in Washington on February 17, 1969, to viewers to apply for station licenses in the District of Columbia. The invitation also seemed to be open in Los Angeles, where a group of citizens, including a dentist, violinist, psychiatrist, and an owner of a chain of women's clothing shops, applied for the KNBC-TV license owned by the National Broadcasting Company, reportedly worth some $75 to $100 million. The stakes are big, but what the FCC has the power to give it also has the power to take away.

FCC licensing power, however, was strong even in the commission's early years. Radio station KVEP of Portland, Oregon, for instance, had its license cancelled in the early 1930s because it permitted a character known as the "Oregon Wildcat" to broadcast "profane" language. Or so he was charged because of his expressions of "damn scoundrel," "by God," and "I'll put on the mantle of the Lord and call down the curse of God on you."[1] Similarly, the commission denied a license renewal to the operator of KTNT, Muscatine, Iowa, who promoted his cancer "cures" and ripped into state medical societies and other opponents. The commission, trying to explain away its censorship, spelled out reasons for its denial:[1]

> This Commission holds no brief for the Medical Associations and other parties whom Mr. Baker does not like. Their alleged sins may be at times of public importance, to be called to the attention of the public over the air in the right way. But this record discloses that Mr. Baker does not do so in any high-minded way. It shows that he continually and erratically, over the air, rides a personal hobby, his cancer-cure ideas and his likes and dislikes of certain persons and things. Surely his infliction of all this on the listeners is not the proper use of a broadcasting license. Many of his utterances are vulgar, if not indeed indecent. Assuredly they are not uplifting or entertaining. Though we may not censor, it is our duty to see that broadcasting licenses do not afford mere personal organs.

Another inhibition on free speech on the air has been the FCC's Mayflower Doctrine. The name of the doctrine stems from the 1940 license renewal application of the Mayflower Broadcasting Corporation for its

---

[1]FCC Docket No. 967, June 5, 1931, quoted in Coase, *op. cit.*, p. 9.

Boston station. During the late 1930s the station broadcast editorials during political campaigns endorsing
some candidates and vetoing others. Also, the station
took stands on questions in public controversy. The FCC
criticized the station but renewed its license after re-
ceiving assurances that the station would not editorialize
in the future. The FCC declared: [1]

> Radio can serve as an instrument of democracy
> only when devoted to the communication of
> information and the exchange of ideas fairly
> and objectively presented. A truly free radio
> cannot be used to advocate the causes of the
> licensee. It cannot be used to support the can-
> didacies of his friends. It cannot be devoted to
> the support of principles he happens to regard
> most favorably. In brief, the broadcaster cannot
> be an advocate.

The Mayflower Doctrine, although clearly an im-
pingement on free speech, stood unchallenged for nine
years until the commission had a change of heart and
modified it in 1959 by substituting the Fairness Doctrine. [2] This "doctrine" sets forth criteria for presenting
both sides of "controversial" issues. "Reasonable opportunity," said the commission, must be allowed to spokes-
men of "responsible positions" on matters of "sufficient
importance."

The Fairness Doctrine has been tested many times.

---

[1] *Mayflower Broadcasting Corp.,* 8 FCC 333 (1940).
[2] *Editorializing by Broadcast Licensees,* 13 FCC 1246, 1250, 1257
(1949).

On April 19, 1963, for example, the commission rejected a petition by Robert H. Scott requesting that renewal of a license for station KNBR, San Francisco, be denied because the station refused him time for a talk in favor of atheism. The FCC told Mr. Scott that although the station offered religious programs it did not broadcast programs directly against him or against the atheistic position. But the latter assertion, in the face of the religious programs cited by Mr. Scott, had a rather hollow ring, especially in light of his earlier petitions and an initial FCC decision in 1946 that his views were indeed controversial and might be entitled to a hearing. But this FCC *obiter dictum* stirred up protests against giving voice to atheism on the airwaves and a congressional committee even investigated the issue. True to the Washington way, the commission backed down on free speech for atheists, and Scott was unable to deny God on the air.

On July 20, 1962, the commission chastised station WOR, New York, for airing a syndicated program entitled "Living Should Be Fun," featuring Dr. Carleton Fredericks, a nutritionist, and for not airing one giving contrary views. The FCC determined that the program included discussions of such "controversial" issues as the fluoridation of water (Dr. Fredericks is an anti-fluoridationist), the value of certain cancer therapy and other treatments, and "views disagreeing with those of public agencies, private organizations, and individuals." Said the commission in part:[2]

---

[1]*29th Annual Report of the Federal Communications Commission,* 1963, p. 58.

Those licensees who rely solely upon the assumed built-in fairness of the program itself or upon the nutritionist's invitation to those with opposing viewpoints cannot be said to have properly discharged their responsibilities. Neither alternative is likely to produce the fairness which the public interest demands. There could be many valid reasons why the advocate of an opposing viewpoint would be unwilling to appear upon such a program. In short, the licensee may not delegate his responsibilities to others, and particularly to an advocate of one particular viewpoint.

To be sure, in determining whether a licensee has made a "reasonable effort" to be fair, the FCC does not automatically substitute its judgment for that of the licensee. Rather, in quasi-judicial hearings, with a number of court trappings, it referees complaints and the licensee's replies before ruling whether the licensee acted reasonably and in good faith. In a complaint cited in the *FCC Annual Report for 1966*,[1] the commission ruled against radio station WGCB in Red Lion, Pennsylvania on a complaint brought by author Fred J. Cook who protested the station's refusal of free air time to reply to a personal attack by Reverend Billy James Hargis on "Christian Crusade," a sponsored right-wing radio show. The radio station argued that it should not be required under the Fairness Doctrine to give free time

---

[1]Pp. 90–91.

to Cook since the attack on him was made in a paid broadcast by Hargis who had previously been the subject of an article in *The Nation* by Cook entitled "Radio Right: Hate Clubs of the Air."

The station was willing to give free time to Mr. Cook on condition he state he was "unable to pay" for the time. The FCC ruled that fairness is not determined by what other media present, but that the station may inquire whether the person attacked is willing to pay for his response or the station may try to find sponsorship for a reply. If these efforts fail, however, the licensee must provide free time for a response. The FCC's stand and its Fairness Doctrine were upheld by the Supreme Court in 1969. In upholding the FCC, the Court somehow struck down the argument that the First Amendment should apply to broadcasters as it does to publishers. The Court affirmed that the air over which broadcasters operate does not belong to them but belongs instead to the "public," and thus the First Amendment was not a sanctuary "for unlimited private censorship operating in a medium not open to all."

The public censorship aspects of the Fairness Doctrine were utilized in 1967 to require stations to include unpaid antismoking "commercials" in their programming to counteract paid commercials for cigarettes. In 1970 the FCC in a bold censorship move banned outright all cigarette commercials from the air. Public censorship could also be involved when such high elected officials as Vice-President Spiro Agnew blast the media—especially radio and TV—for a supposed domination of public opinion with one-sided anti-Adminis-

tration views. Implicit in the criticism is the possibility
of regulatory retaliation against any media dependent
upon the government for existence. Again, Senator
John A. Pastore of Rhode Island, chairman of the Senate Communications Subcommittee, in 1969 called on
the FCC commissioners to testify on programming,
"particularly the treatment of violence and sex." Said
the senator:[1]

> The most cataclysmic thing in America today is
> television. We've got to clean it up. The indus-
> try has not lived up to its responsibility and it
> has not kept the promises it made to me. If it
> doesn't exercise restraint, drastic action will be
> taken.

Related to the Fairness Doctrine is the Equal Time
Doctrine (Section 315[a] of the FCC Act) which
stipulates that if one qualified candidate for political
office receives free air time, all other candidates must
receive equal time. This means, of course, that if broadcasters give free time to the candidates of the two major
parties, they must, as a rule, also give free time to candidates of such parties as the Prohibition, Vegetarian,
Socialist, etc.

Section 315 (a) comes before Congress for suspension quadrennially as presidential elections loom on the
horizon. It was suspended with bipartisan support for
the 1960 elections which permitted TV debates between
candidates Kennedy and Nixon and left out some

---

[1]*New York Times,* March 5, 1969.

twenty-two other candidates. These debates, however, seemed to cool the ardor of at least the front-runners in later presidential election polls so congressional votes for suspension were hard to find in 1964 and 1968. In 1968 front-runner Richard M. Nixon said he would like to debate Hubert H. Humphrey, but not if it meant giving free TV exposure to George Wallace.

Also related to the Fairness Doctrine is the Overcommercialization Doctrine first promulgated in 1963 when by a four to three decision the FCC sought to limit the number of commercials broadcast by a radio or TV station. The commission proposed to base its commercial-limiting rules on those included in the Code of the National Association of Broadcasters—roughly eight minutes per hour of prime TV evening time—but would not be bound by such rules. To forestall any limitation, Representative Walter Rogers, chairman of the House Interstate and Foreign Commerce Committee, introduced a bill to deny the FCC commercial-limiting power. In 1964 the House passed the Rogers Bill 317 to 43. But by then the FCC, seeing the handwriting on the wall, backed down on the overcommercialization issue, save to say it would continue to check on a case-to-case basis. However, a later *Annual Report of the FCC* said the commission would continue to proceed against "loud" commercials, although it concedes that it is not a simple matter for the FCC to control decibels.

The overcommercialization issue touches on freedom of enterprise as well as on freedom of speech and press. Free enterprise means under the broad base of law, freedom from outside control. It means a seller—in this case a broadcaster—is essentially free to offer his services on any terms whatsoever, providing of course libel, slander, fraud, or misrepresentation are not involved. It also means the buyer is free to accept or reject that offer. And in the case of radio or TV, the listener or viewer—the consumer—is free to turn to competing communications media such as books, newspapers, magazines, movies, etc., or to turn a dial, flick a switch, or simply ignore excessive or loud commercials and stations. Out of competitive necessity, broadcasters and advertisers themselves tend to seek to limit commercials for fear of driving away business. As Robert Moses told a New York luncheon of the International Radio and Television Society:[1]

> In your efforts to impress childish minds with trade names you can find to a decibel precisely when repetition becomes so annoying as to be intolerable. It's a dubious and dangerous game. In time the victims may not swallow it. They may throw up. Gentlemen, beware! The worm may turn. The victim, if you irritate him enough, has a deadly weapon against you. He can simply tune you out.

Still, for all their concern about "excessive" commercialization, the commissioners have long dragged their feet whenever the question of authorizing commercial-less pay-TV comes before the FCC. Pay-TV could provide a cultural mecca in Mr. Minow's waste-

---

[1]*Wall Street Journal,* April 28, 1964.

land—Broadway plays and musicals, the Metropolitan Opera "live" from New York, lectures by historians and philosophers, and so on, as well as first-run movies, sports events, and other ventures. The FCC, to be sure, authorized pay-TV technical tests in 1950, but in obedience to the Washington way it allowed itself to be influenced by a number of powerful congressmen, entrenched broadcasters, and vocal motion picture exhibitors into at most a half-hearted stance in favor of pay-TV. It was not until 1959 that the FCC invited applications for three-year trial operations over TV stations and not until 1962 that the first trial got started over WHCT-TV, Hartford, Connecticut.

Finally, in 1968 the FCC flashed a flickering green light to pay-TV and broadcast competition. It ruled that pay-TV be restricted to markets where at least four "free" TV stations were already operating. It further ruled that pay-TV could not telecast any non-reserved seat movie less than two years old or any sports event which had been regularly available on "free" TV.

Competition is much to be desired, but the problem here is that the competitive battle between "free" TV and pay-TV has not been fought by the rules of competition that prevail, or should prevail, in a free market with full freedom of entry. Pay-TV has never been allowed by the FCC to enter the market on anything like a broad scale, never been permitted broadly to succeed or fail on its own merits, under its own handicap of having to charge hard cash in competition with "free" TV, never been permitted a real opportunity to make money or lose money for its financial risk-takers.

Another competitive threat to the established broad-casters is wired TV—community antenna television (CATV). CATV depends on cable rather than broad-cast transmission and thus escaped FCC regulation for a number of years. But to conform to the Washington way, the FCC began asserting its authority in 1966 over this electronic entry to the American living room—an authority sustained by the U.S. Court of Appeals.

CATV started out innocently enough, as far the FCC and the licensed TV stations were concerned, by pro-viding reception to otherwise unreachable rural or poor-reception areas via master antennas which pick up distant TV signals and relay them through cable to homes subscribing to the service. But CATV, fed by fees from satisfied subscribers, began to grow—there are now thousands of CATV stations in the country—and to move in on the licensed TV stations. Once it dawned on FCC licensees that programs could be imported from one city to another even over substantial distances by cable, they became annoyed with the competition.

Two TV stations in San Diego, California, pleaded for FCC cease and desist orders to CATV operators, Mission Cable TV, Inc. and Poway (San Diego), who were relaying Los Angeles programs to San Diego. And in Ohio, Buckeye Cablevision, Inc. of Toledo was also accused of poaching on FCC-staked out TV territory. Both cases resulted in FCC cease and desist orders against the CATV stations.

So the least the pay-TV and CATV stories reveal is that the FCC, like virtually every other regulatory agency, tenderly tries to shield its industry from the harsh winds of competition. Certainly there is no jamming of the airwaves by CATV, which was the FCC's raison d'être for regulating broadcasters in the first place. And certainly pay-TV could provide alternatives to "wasteland" programming and could even assuage the FCC's fears of overcommercialization. It appears that the FCC is simply protecting its licensees, reestablishing the point that a regulatory authority tends to be an arm of those it supposedly regulates.

So, again, consider the basic question: Is this regulation necessary? If it isn't, many of broadcasting's problems such as politics and loss of freedom of speech and press would not be so evident. Of course, other media have their share of problems relating to politics and competition but nowhere to the extent of the broadcasters. The reason for this difference lies in the FCC's licensing power. Were newspapers or magazines licensed, it follows that freedom of the press would likely be limited under a Fairness Doctrine similar to that which governs the broadcasters.

Officially the answer to the question of regulatory necessity is that broadcasting laissez faire was tried and found sadly wanting, that the government had to move in with its licensing power to allocate available frequencies and prevent interference by one broadcaster in the frequency of another. The FCC points out, correctly, that the available frequencies are in short supply, especially in key market areas. The frequency spectrum, according to one estimate, permits only 106 AM radio frequencies, 50 FM frequencies, 12 VHF television channels, and 70 UHF channels, if there is to be no interference. However, across the continent, with stations widely separated and transmission powers low enough, literally thousands of AM and FM radio stations and VHF and UHF television stations can and do coexist.

Yet even conceding the sharp limitation on the number of stations or the fact that there are many more potential users than available air space does not make the licensing argument valid. Every valuable commodity is in relatively scarce supply. Indeed, it is scarcity which helps to give value to the commodity. It follows, then, that the rationing of radio and TV frequencies could be treated as are other scarce resources—that is, rationing through the impersonal market mechanism. One approach has been suggested by Professor R. H. Coase of the University of Chicago.[1] Professor Coase observes, as did Professor Jaffe, that the property rights in radio frequencies and especially in TV channels are of great value, frequently in the millions of dollars for each station.

The plan of Professor Coase comes down, in essence, to this: let present commercial broadcast licensees acquire permanent property rights to their present frequencies, permitting them to sell or lease them, or acquire additional frequencies from others; let the government auction off the property rights in remaining frequencies to the highest bidders; and thus enable the

---

[1]See his article "The Federal Communications Commission," *The Journal of Law and Economics,* October 1959.

FCC to get entirely out of the commercial licensing—and censorship—business.

Of course, under this market mechanism, Americans would no longer "own the air," but then they never really did. While still under antitrust, as discussed earlier, broadcasters would no longer be under the ephemeral "trustee" image that the FCC has long sought to create. Also, windfall profits from FCC favoritism for this license applicant or that would evaporate.

Critics of the Coase impersonal market plan may argue that such a suggestion would simply award frequencies to those most able to afford them. This of course is true. The price mechanism—admittedly imperfect but, in my judgment, the least imperfect in an imperfect world—shifts resources to those entrepreneurs who can apply them according to the demonstrated preferences of the public. Granted, consumer taste may leave something—or a great deal—to be desired, but with freedom of entry for CATV and pay-TV, minority tastes could be well served. And the FCC's broadcast licensing power could be phased out of existence.

CHAPTER IX

The Case
for Deregulation

Underlying most arguments against the free
market is a lack of belief in freedom itself.
—Milton Friedman
Capitalism and Freedom

As was noted in the preface, man needs government.
But practically everyone agrees with that statement.
The questions are what kind of government and how
much. Government by interventionistic regulation, as
demonstrated in this study, leaves much to be desired.
It will be recalled that, at the outset, a distinction was
made between interventionistic regulation, which is
detrimental to competition and economic growth, and
neutral or benign regulation, which is either helpful to
competition and growth or at least not harmful to it.

One area where neutral or benign regulation can
prove helpful is in the area of maximizing the quality

of the environment and minimizing the harmful side effects of the affluent society. For, unfortunately, all too often the affluent society is an effluent society. This need not be the case—and increasingly is not the case—as problems of ecology are recognized and pollution alleviated. For example, on a rather grand scale we see London and Pittsburgh no longer shrouded in smoke and smog.

On perhaps a less grand but more individual scale, we see sanitation improved: bathtubs are standard, outhouses are gone, water is chlorinated, milk is pasteurized—and we see medicine becoming more preventative, land being set aside for recreation and culture, birth as well as death rates falling. We have, in short, come part way in improving the environment.

Yet much remains to be done in the area of pollution control: Dumps deface the countryside; planes emit noise; autos and trucks spew fumes; individuals, industries, and governments pollute rivers, lakes and air with wastes. Here benign regulation by government—with industry's technical counsel can set environmental standards and, importantly, provide legal penalties for noncompliance with such standards. Standards, however, cannot be hastily and arbitrarily set, for environmental technology has not yet arrived at a stage of development or production where pollution can be summarily banished. To improve our air, for example, automobile engines and fuel require redesign, smokestacks require effective emission traps; to improve our waters, waste treatment requires improved filter and chemical installations. All this will take time. It will also take money—

a cost ultimately borne by the consumer in the form of higher prices to cover the costs of improved technology in the products he buys and in higher taxes to cover the costs of improved environmental services in the community in which he lives.

The money, provided benign environmental regulation is not converted into interventionistic regulation, can be considered well spent. For, as we include social costs and neighborhood effects in the price system, conservation behavior and technological improvement tend to follow, to the betterment of the environment. But these effects still lend themselves to the guideposts of Peter Drucker in his *Age of Discontinuity*,[1] where he cautions "let government govern and the private sector do." In other words, let regulation be benign by setting reasonable governmental-industry standards—with teeth —for the environment and let business innovate within these standards, within the free enterprise system.

The basic regulatory problem, then, is not with benign regulation; it is with anticompetitive regulation, the type held here to be interventionistic, and well described by a *Fortune* writer as a "mess."[2] The whole idea of regulation in the beginning was to cure what interventionists claimed was an unregulated "mess," and certainly not to create a new one. The regulatory agencies, especially those dubbed as "independent" by Congress, were designed to preserve the free enterprise

---

[1] Harper & Row, 1969.
[2] George Bookman, "Regulation by Elephant, Rabbit and Lark," *Fortune,* June 1961.

system and sound business management, while at the same time supposedly correcting the alleged "abuses" and "excesses" that gave rise to the regulatory agencies in the first place. To further the laudable goal of correction, the word of the regulators was made law—administrative law, in the phrase of Roscoe Pound.

Accordingly, the regulators somehow combine quasi-legislative, quasi-judicial, and administrative authority, with few checks and balances. Ubiquitiously they make rules and directives, issue orders and regulations, grant franchises and licenses, sign cease and desist orders, levy penalties, award damages, and require persons and companies to perform or not perform certain acts. Some of these regulatory actions, such as the awarding of a TV channel or an airline route, involve grants of great wealth. This wealth can be negative as well as positive. Recently members of a union in a Wisconsin factory had to pay fines for exceeding production quotas laid down by the union. Some fines amounted to one hundred dollars for "persistent and flagrant" quota violations. The NLRB upheld the fines.

Obviously such interventionistic regulation is government of men, not of law; and appeal to the courts for legal redress is frequently hard, expensive, or out of the question. FCC Commissioner Lee Loevinger sensed the regulatory dilemma of administrative law in his dissenting opinion in FCC Docket 16258 on the commission's denial of AT&T's cost allocations in some telephone proceedings. Commissioner Loevinger declared in part:

It seems to me quite improper . . . to mingle the functions of investigator, prosecutor, advocate, ex parte confidential advisor, and adjudicator. Each time that the Common Carrier Bureau leaves the hearing room as a party and enters the conference room to act as a judge in the same matter that it has been litigating it further offends the standards of propriety which I believe, and which the Administrative Conference of the United States has declared, should govern proceedings such as this.

Consider more fully the problem of the regulatory commission or board member serving as judge—i.e., taking over a judicial function. One of the striking characteristics and real protections of the federal judiciary—life tenure—is denied to the nominally "independent" regulatory commissioners. The federal judge, at least in theory, can devote himself to disinterested and nonpartisan application and intepretation of the law; but the regulatory agency member is in the frequent dilemma of the short-term appointee caught somewhere between hoped-for reappointment in the agency he serves or possibly landing in an executive suite of the industry he regulates. The regulator by and large has to "get along" with his party and President and his regulated industry or sector. The President, whatever his party, would generally rather not appoint or reappoint what the regulated industry regards as an uncooperative regulator or regulator-to-be.

So the regulator usually becomes a "nice guy"— practically a servant of the regulatees: The NLRB member tends to be a servant of the unions, the CAB member of the scheduled airlines, and so on, with the consumer interest generally lost in the shuffle.

Compounding their problems, the regulators are supposed to provide industrial leadership, to be industry experts, to administer complex business problems with justice and dispatch, all in businesslike fashion. But, by the very nature of their mandate from Congress to intervene, by their very mission to contravene the free market, by their insulation from investors on the one hand and consumers on the other, the regulators—however able, hardworking, and constructive-minded they may be—cannot help but make business less businesslike, less adaptable to accelerating technology and other dynamic supply-and-demand conditions. And this widening gap between the normative world of the regulator and the real world of the regulated industry is a problem that has snowballed since 1887, the year of the birth of the ICC, that must snowball even more as the dynamics of the marketplace and the underlying conditions that originally occasioned a particular regulatory agency shift rapidly into entirely different conditions.

Consider just the attempt of regulators to set prices, from, say, the Department of Agriculture establishing the support price of soybeans to the ICC determining the price of transporting by rail a carload of the same soybeans from the Midwest to the East Coast. In each case the regulators attempt not only to gauge the market forces of supply and demand but also to gauge such distinctly nonmarket criteria as a congressionally-required "balanced national transportation system" and "parity between farm and nonfarm prices," as prevailed in the 1909–1914 period.

Resource misallocation and other traumatic repercussions are well-nigh inevitable under such conditions. These conditions are compounded by an inevitable information lag and a bureaucratic labyrinth. As F. A. Hayek pointed out in his article on "The Use of Knowledge in Society,"[1] government centralization compounds the information problem by multiplying and lengthening the channels of information. Bureaucratic procedures further delay and distort the flow of critical data. The result is that the regulators can never quite know, despite voluminous reporting procedures, just what should be the right policies for production, marketing, finance, engineering, research, etc., for their respective industries or sectors.

Another complication—and cost—of regulation and, indeed, of our regulated society is time-consuming paperwork—reports, applications, questionnaires, tax returns, subpoenas, orders, directives, rulings, legal opinions, appeals from orders, and so on. The paperwork springs from the diverse and complex decisions that the regulators must make. Fixed criteria are elusive. On-the-spot reactions are generally lacking. Data, lots of it, must be in regulatory hand; paper, lots of it, must be signed, witnessed, authorized, notarized. Who merits, for example, an award of a television channel in Miami, Florida? What constitutes mass picketing at a silver mine in Coeur d'Alene, Idaho? How much should be the support price of long-staple cotton in the southwestern United States? Does a merger between the ABC

---

[1] *American Economic Review, September* 1945, pp. 519–530.

Co. and the XYZ Corp. "substantially lessen" competition? Etc. Etc.

This diversion of market decision-making through
the sluggish maze of the Washington way produces an
inevitable "regulatory lag," a lag that can run into
years. The sorry tale of the Rutland Railway is a case
in point. This little Vermont line sought to go out of
business in 1961, three months after it had been struck
by its unions; the ICC took one full year of consideration before it at last decided that the Rutland's request
should be granted, with the Rutland's losses by then
compounded. A recent White House study group reported that the average ICC time needed to rule on a
transportation rate case is eighteen months; the average
time for the NLRB on a routine unfair labor charge is
a little better, 11.5 months. But if such regulation is
unnecessary—and most of it is—then all this time is lost
time, a blunting of managerial decision-making, a drag
on the economy.

The time lapse has a way of becoming even longer.
One drug industry executive told *U.S. News and World
Report*[1] that the average time for an application for a
new drug to be processed by the Food and Drug Administration was 106 days in 1958, 327 days in 1963,
and more than 600 days in 1968.

Or consider the Federal Power Commission. When,
thanks to the Supreme Court ruling in *Phillips Petro-
leum* v. *Wisconsin,*[2] the FPC undertook to fix prices of

---

[1]March 3, 1969.
[2]347 U.S. 672 (1954).

natural gas all the way back to the wellhead, an early estimate of the time required to complete the price-fixing mission was from four to fourteen years. In 1960, in a report to President-Elect Kennedy, Judge James Landis charged that "the Federal Power Commission without question represents the outstanding example in the Federal government of the breakdown of the administrative process."[1] In 1964, a Senate subcommittee investigating the natural-gas regulatory operations of the FPC criticized one especially ponderous FPC questionnaire. The questionnaire, said to weigh ten pounds, was defended by the commission as necessary to gather data on which to establish a formula for area price regulation of natural gas. In 1965, the FPC decided upon maximum prices for the first of twenty-three gas-producing areas, the Permian Basin of Texas and New Mexico. The commission added in its announcement on prices that its price ceiling would be frozen for two and one-half years, presumably while it turned its attention to the twenty-two other producing areas. Yet, would supply and demand lie dormant for two and one-half years? Hardly. The bureaucratic upshot is less gas at higher cost—and a gas shortage in 1970–71 instead of more gas at lower cost—to the detriment of the Forgotten Man, just as he is similarly nicked to the tune of some $5 billion annually by oil import quotas.

Still, given the heavy work loads and the built-in bureaucratic procedures of the agencies, it is a tribute

---

[1] James M. Landis, *Report on Regulatory Agencies to the Preisdent-Elect* 1960, p. 53.

to the regulators that the regulatory lag is not even greater. One FPC commissioner, for example, reported that he helped make eighteen thousand case decisions over a five-year period, or an average of about fourteen decisions per working day, each decision involving voluminous suporting data and documents. Little wonder, then, that the regulators find it practically impossible to keep up with work loads that seem to be increasing every year under elaborate procedures imposed by court decisions and Congress, including the Administrative Procedures Act of 1946.

These procedural complexities include adversary proceedings, cross-examination of witnesses, rebuttals, rules of evidence, technical objections, appeals, etc. The procedural requirement that commissioners must record their reasoning behind each factor considered in every decision, and also behind the disposition of every exception filed, makes for still more time-consuming paperwork. These procedures were designed to protect individual rights from arbitrary administrative action and are thus most laudable, but they do not get to the heart of the regulatory problem—interventionism, the substitution of the Washington way for the market way.

Delay, however, is but one part of the regulatory story. Politics is another. The political climate naturally has vast influence on administrative law. As noted, regulators are political appointees usually and understandably seeking reappointment. The politics of regulation is further sharpened by the presence of litigants, applicants, interveners, organized trade groups, lobbyists of

every description, and individually affected businessmen, all seeking directly or indirectly to influence the
decision-making of the agencies—and the Congress. As
Senator Everett Dirksen of Illinois explained his own
agency-intervening:[1]

> I think that is a part of my job in a ponderous
> government with two and a half million people
> on the payroll, and agencies all over the lot,
> where the average citizen becomes thoroughly
> bewildered.

To be sure, businessmen have long sung hosannas and
made obeisances to competition at practically every
business convention and luncheon—while they frequently
have at the same time sought ways and means to under-
cut the market forces of supply and demand with private evasions or pressure for public regulation. The
private evasions might consist of pools, cartels, gentlemen's agreements, and other collusive arrangements.
Public regulation includes franchises, licenses, tariffs,
quotas, building codes, and regulatory bodies all too often
ready, willing, and able to do pretty much as many an
organized industry asks.

With such problems, we should ask, "Why a regulatory agency in the first place?" Scholars of the caliber

---

[1]Bookman, *op. cit.*, p. 138.

of Robert E. Cushman,[1] Marver H. Bernstein,[2] Dudley F. Pegrum,[3] Donald Stevenson Watson,[4] Milton Friedman,[5] and Asher Isaacs and Reuben S. Slesinger[6] have looked into the pros and cons of the regulatory problem. These and other academicians generally see the pros of a regulatory agency in terms of its expertise, a body which can assist Congress in the formation of regulatory policy, a tribunal which can adjudicate the conflicting interests of producer against producer and producer against consumer. These scholars also recognize some cons of regulation—politics, inefficiency, and possible impropriety.

For example, Dean Bernstein of Princeton's Woodrow Wilson School of Public Administration concluded in 1955 that the regulatory commissions "have failed to keep abreast of industrial and technological developments. Consequently, the regulatory mechanism has an air of obsolescence."[7] More recently, Dean Bernstein has declared: "I think in many areas, we've simply outgrown the situations that brought regulation."[8] Domestic air service is a case in point. Dr. Bernstein noted that

---

[1] Robert E. Cushman, *The Independent Regulatory Commissions,* Oxford, 1941.
[2] Marver H. Bernstein, *Regulating Business by Independent Commission,* Princeton, 1955.
[3] Dudley F. Pegrum, *Public Regulation of Business,* Irwin, 1959.
[4] Donald Stevenson Watson, *Economic Policy: Business and Government,* Houghton Mifflin, 1960.
[5] Milton Friedman, *Capitalism and Freedom,* Chicago, 1962.
[6] Asher Isaacs and Reuben E. Slesinger, *Business, Government, and Public Policy,* Van Nostrand, 1964.
[7] Bernstein, *op. cit.,* p. 100.
[8] *Nation's Business,* January 1965, p. 36.

the CAB was designed originally to aid the fledgling air transport industry; today that industry is strong enough to bear a good deal of deregulation of rates, routes, and other nonsafety aspects.

Professor Friedman of the University of Chicago goes further in his critique of regulation. Distinguishing among the three "evils" of private monopoly, public monopoly, and public regulation, he concludes that, if tolerable, "private monopoly may be the least of the evils."[1] Professor Friedman stresses the dynamic nature of competition, the fact that private monopoly is generally short-lived, that in the illustrative case of the railroads and the ICC, pipelines, bargelines, trucklines, and airlines have long provided competition galore but the ICC, conceived on the monopoly theory of railroads, goes on and on, to the detriment of the railroads' competitiveness.

Professor George Stigler of the University of Chicago has also wondered about the efficacy of regulation. In an article entitled "Public Regulation of the Securities Market," published in the April 1964 issue of *The Journal of Business,* he concluded that, on the basis of statistical comparisons of new stock issues, both before and after the establishment of the Securities and Exchange Commission, SEC registration requirements have had no significant effect on the quality of new securities sold to the public. In other words, the investing public is as vulnerable today as ever. Too, in another article, Professor Stigler investigated the effects of state utility

---

[1]Friedman, *op. cit.,* p. 28.

regulation on electrical rates in the U.S. Dr. Stigler found little evidence that regulation has in fact lowered the cost of electricity to consumers.[1]

So, again, is regulation necessary? The answer depends in part on one's definition of competition. Competition, according to one influential school of thought, is little different from the Hobbesian description of primitive life—"solitary, poor, nasty, brutish, and short." In this view competition is the law of the jungle. It is cutthroat, dog-eat-dog, man's-inhumanity-to-man, or, to use the phrase in the Communist Manifesto, "naked, shameless, direct, brutal exploitation." Again, from another but more influential view, with the exception of wheat farming and a few other lines of endeavor which qualify as "pure" competition, ordinary competition is "imperfect," "monopolistic," or "oligopolistic." These are hardly terms of approbation. Instead, they signify the existence of market conditions and opportunities favorable to collusion, price-rigging, market allocation, administered pricing, monopoly gains, and other assumed predatory behavior detrimental to the interests of the consumer.

The prevailing definition of competition has been importantly influenced by the depression-born thinking of Edward H. Chamberlin of Hardvard University[2] and Mrs. Joan Robinson of Cambridge University,[3] who

---

[1]George J. Stigler and C. Friedland, "What Can Regulators Regulate?: The Case of Electricity," *The Journal of Law and Economics,* October 1962.

[2]Edward H. Chamberlin, *The Theory of Monopolistic Competition,* Harvard, 1933.

[3]Joan Robinson, *The Economics of Imperfect Competition,* Macmillan, 1933.

saw competition as usually weak and ineffectual. One upshot of this negative view is that the language of competition has been encumbered by adjectives, many of which betray a hard or jaded view of business trade. As Fritz Machlup of Princeton University as observed, competitive terminology employs such adjective as:[1]

> fair, sharp, keen, fierce, brutal, unfair, destructive, ruinous, cutthroat, free, atomistic, pure, perfect, effective, unrestricted, simple, complete, homogeneous, rigorous, unmitigated, restrained, restricted, limited, incomplete, modified, cautious, considerate, cooperative, intermediate, hybrid, monopolistic, imperfect, heterogeneous, friendly, civilized, oligopolistic, controlled, regulated, discriminatory, predatory, potential, and workable.

Economists are not alone in adversely influencing the intellectual climate for competition; novelists, historians, and politicians such as Ida Tarbell, Theodore Dreiser, Upton Sinclair, Matthew Josephson, the Temporary National Economic Committee, and Senator Estes Kefauver also got into the act of criticizing the lack of competition, of seeing monopolistic tendencies in virtually every executive suite, of seeking public control over perfectly normal competitive situations.

Witness, for example, public control over taxicabs in many of the leading cities of America. In New York, for instance, where the city fixes fares and the number of

---

[1]Fritz Machlup, *The Economics of Sellers' Competition,* Johns Hopkins, 1952.

cabs on the streets, the taxicab shortage and general surliness of service are sore points with New Yorkers. A taxicab license—visible as a medallion on the side of the cab—costs a monopoly price in excess of $20 thousand, an amount well beyond the reach of the average cabbie who might like to go into business for himself.

Yet the assumption that "monopoly" and "oligopoly" are rife in America just does not hold water. As Professor Warren Nutter of the University of Virginia noted:[1]

> It makes sense to say that competition is the normal condition in our economy. Theory should be brought in touch with the world we live in by recasting monopolistic elements in their proper role: as a special, not a general case.

Nonetheless, regulation of the interventionistic type supposedly coping with "incipient" monopoly mushrooms. Why? Milton Friedman has suggested some general answers in his *Capitalism and Freedom*. He points, for example, to the argument of A. V. Dicey to be found in Dicey's lectures on the relation between law and public opinion. Dicey raised the question of why England turned away from individualism and toward collectivism beginning in the latter part of the nineteenth century when freedom and free enterprise had succeeded in markedly raising living standards. One of Dicey's points is that the case for intervention is very

---

[1]American Economic Association, *Proceedings,* May 1954, p. 76.

simple, while the case for nonintervention is extremely subtle. How easy it is to see that there is something not quite right in the body economic, that the cure is simply a matter of passing a law. Farm prices are too low, cries the farm bloc; so pass a law supporting them. The difficulty of meeting the argument for the use of law when the direct consequences are there for all to see is plain; farm prices are indeed raised; but the indirect consequences of subsidies, surpluses, controls, etc. are generally long-run, complex, diffused, and imperfectly perceived. Thus, to cite another example, the people are quick to see how a tariff will protect an industry and save jobs; they do not readily perceive the jobs lost in exports and the heightened cost of living. Consider, for example, the additional pennies per gallon of gasoline imposed on the consumer by the government's oil import quota policy—a policy established in the name of "national defense" but eagerly sought by the domestic oil producers. A similar story could be told about the government's sugar policy, which protects domestic producers, and imposes additional pennies per pound of sugar on the Forgotten Man.

Friedman also notes that another aspect of the interventionist problem of democracy was suggested by Wesley Mitchell in his essay on *The Backward Art of Spending Money.* Mitchell noted the profound difference between the interests of people as consumers and their interests as producers, with the upshot of differing and most uncoordinated political pressure bearing on legislators to "do something," to regulate Industry X and control Sector Y. Generally the producers are or-

ganized and the consumers unorganized; so what the
producers "gain" from regulation, the consumers lose.
The irony, however, is that every producer is necessarily
a consumer—and vice versa. Thus, in the final accounting, apart from some government subsidized or otherwise rewarded regulatees, there are no winners: The
losses wash out the "gains" and then some.

The further irony is that, after the pressure lets up
and even after the "need" dies down, the regulation
goes on. As Peter Drucker observed in his *Age of Discontinuity*, the inability to stop a program, even a useless
one, is the central degenerative disease of government
and a major factor accounting for the sickness of
government today. Mr. Drucker related the discovery
of the "Halifax Disaster Commission," still operating in
Nova Scotia, by the Royal Commission of the Government of Canada. The Royal Commission, taking an in-
ventory of all Canadian government agencies in 1967,
was astounded to find the Halifax agency still copying
the records of relief payments made forty years earlier
to the victims of a 1917 explosion of an ammunition
vessel in Halifax harbor. More recently the Nixon Administration sought, unsuccessfully, to eliminate the
Federal Board of Tea Tasters, a long-lived if miniscule
bureaucracy costing $125 thousand a year and author-
ized by the Tea Importation Act of 1897.

This Parkinsonian longevity of bureaucracies can be
traced in large measure to the noncost-recouping nature
of government, its lack of a profit motive, its basic un-
responsiveness to price signals and consumer sovereignty

—all of which bear on the nature of bureaucracy and of regulation. In addition, regulation suffers from soft corruptibility—the temptations of extra-"friendly" government-business relations, of what President Eisenhower called, when he left office, the "military-industrial complex." Little wonder, then, at the widespread disenchantment with interventionistic government today, even behind the Iron Curtain.

Peter Drucker was certainly correct in his observation that modern government is, universally, bloated and sick from a swelling and generally ineffective public sector. It follows that the great need throughout the world is for the reprivatization of many public undertakings and the deregulation of many regulated private enterprises.

In fact, local undertakings have been privatized—even police and fire protection. On police protection, for example, the protective security industry claims that two out of every three security officers in the country are employed by private groups or firms. A private corporation in Arizona fights fires for profit and provides protection over a four hundred-mile area in cities such as Scottsdale and Yuma. Education is being widely privatized. Private school enrollments have nearly doubled in the last decade. Increasingly private "performance contractors" such as Westinghouse Learning Corporation and Singer Greflex are being hired by public school systems to take over remedial classes. In fact, remedial classes in an entire school district in Gary, Indiana, have been handed over to an educational contractor who has guaranteed that he will teach the students to read or forfeit his pay. Garbage collection is privatized in Seattle and San Francisco.

This turning to the private sector for public services evidences dissatisfaction with the public way of providing community needs and the search for a better way. Bureaucracies have been found wanting in efficiency and lack the discipline of the profit motive to prod them into efficiency. Regulatory agencies, in particular, can not keep pace with the dynamism of the market. As Phillip Elman said when he retired as an FTC commissioner in 1970:

> I have come to the view that the chronic unresponsiveness and basic deficiencies in agency performance are largely rooted in its organic structure and will not be cured by minor or transient personnel or procedural improvements. It is time for radical structural reform.

Deregulation and reprivatization are not an argument for weak and ineffectual government. They are simply a recognition of the efficacy of the market, of the inherent incompatibility between economics and politics, of the built-in shortcomings of government intervention. This recognition would include, as discussed in the previous chapters, the phasing-out of the FDA, FTC, NLRB, ICC, FCC (broadcast licensing power only), CAB, and the interventionistic functions of the Antitrust Division. Deregulation and reprivatization, however must be accompanied by a revitalization of the federal and state judicial systems which would, as noted in previous chapters, absorb the contract-adjudication and consumer-protection functions of the phased-out agencies.

But the judiciary, like the rest of government, is sick. In fiscal 1968, the median time between filing a complaint and the start-up of a civil trial in a federal case was forty months in the Southern District of New York and the Eastern District of Pennsylvania, and seventy-seven months in the Southern District of California. In other words, for justice to even get a chance to triumph in a federal court, it takes more than three years on the East Coast and six years on the West Coast. Little wonder, then, that in 1970 Chief Justice Warren Burger likened the federal judiciary to "a merchant trying to operate a cracker-barrel corner grocery store with the methods and equipment of 1900."[1] Accordingly, he put forward suggestions to streamline the judicial procedure and expand the number of judgeships.

In sum, free enterprise—the consumer's best servant—is being smothered by interventionistic regulation. Much of this regulation marches under the banner of consumerism. Still, consumerism has a constructive role to play, but it can be pushed too far, limiting individual freedom and harming the consumer's interest. Consumerists can and should educate, yet they should be wary of shifting from consumer sovereignty in the marketplace to government sovereignty, however benevolent that government is deemed to be. Consumerists should see that

---

[1] Address, American Bar Association, St. Louis, Mo., August 10, 1970.

government sovereignty in the marketplace tends to be transmuted into producer sovereignty, stifling freedom of entry and, indeed, freedom of enterprise itself. They should agree with Professor Yale Brozen of the University of Chicago Graduate School of Business, who noted that "free enterprise in this country is one-quarter dead and one-quarter strangled—only half alive."[1] Accordingly, they should push for the deregulation and reprivatization of the American consumer.

Government should govern. It should help lead in a pluralistic society. It should help set a moral tone in that society. It should help provide justice. It should protect society—"life, liberty or property," in the phrase of the Fifth and Fourteenth Amendments—from within and from without. It should help preserve freedom. To this end, while preserving benign regulation, an enlightened government and citizenry should progressively deregulate our regulated society and re-enthrone the consumer in the marketplace.

---

[1]*Barron's,* August 10, 1970.

A Publication
of the Principles
# of Freedom Committee

The great body of economic and political literature since World War II—both academic and popular—has presented a misleading picture of the performance of private enterprise and of the State in the economies of the free world. This literature exaggerates the defects of the one and the merits of the other. Freedom will remain in jeopardy unless the public gains a clearer picture of the workings of the free market and comes to realize that its greatest virtue is not its extraordinary capacity to produce widely diffused material benefits, important as this merit is, but its unique capacity to protect the great immaterial values of our Western Heritage.

As a means of increasing the flow of literature that would correct the picture and strengthen the foundations of freedom, a group calling itself the Principles of Freedom Committee was formed during the early 1960s to promote a series of books dealing with important economic and political issues of the day. To assist in the international publication and distribution of the books, the Committee recruited an advisory group of scholars from sixteen countries. *The Regulated Consumer* is the fifth book in the Principles of Freedom Series.

The membership of the Committee has changed over the years through retirements and replacements by co-option. The original members were Professors Milton Friedman, F. A. Hayek, G. Warren Nutter, B. A. Rogge, and John V. Van Sickle, Executive Secretary; Ruth Sheldon Knowles, Project Coordinator; and Byron K. Trippet, Committee Member Ex-Officio. Dr. Trippet retired in 1965 following his resignation as President of Wabash College. Professors Hayek and Nutter retired in 1968, and three new members were added: Gottfried Haberler, Galen L. Stone Professor of International Trade, Harvard University; F. A. Harper, President, Institute for Humane Studies; and Don Paarlberg, Hillenbrand Professor of Agricultural Economics, Purdue University. In 1970 Gottfried Dietze, Professor of Political Science at The Johns Hopkins University, joined the Committee, and Kenneth S. Templeton, Jr., assumed the duties of Executive Secretary from Dr. Van Sickle.

The original Committee requested modest nonrecurring grants from a number of corporations and foundations. These donors receive copies of all books as they appear, and their help in promoting the distribution of the books is welcomed. The Institute for Humane Studies handles the funds received from the project's supporters and issues annual reports. Decisions as to authors, subjects, and acceptability of manuscripts rest exclusively with the Committee.

Earlier volumes in the Principles of Freedom Series are:

Great Myths of Economics (1968) by Don Paarlberg

The Strange World of Ivan Ivanov (1969 by
    G. Warren Nutter)

Freedom in Jeopardy: The Tyranny of Idealism
    (1969) by John V. Van Sickle

The Genius of the West (1971) by Louis Rougier

Index

Name Index

Subject Index